MODERN COMPETITION
AND BUSINESS POLICY

MODERN COMPETITION AND BUSINESS POLICY

BY

H. S. DENNISON

AND

J.K.GALBRAITH

OXFORD UNIVERSITY PRESS

NEW YORK

1938

Foreword

FOR *many generations business men, politicians, and economists have looked upon the economic system much as a physician looks upon a normally constituted man. Such a man is expected to be sick occasionally, in fact a certain amount of sickness is considered almost inevitable. But ill health is not supposed to be his normal condition. In much the same way it has been supposed that, while there might be in the economy occasional periods of depression or of ill health, the normal condition was one of well-being or prosperity.*

The analogy may be extended to the matter of treatment. When a man is sick there is a general disposition among physicians to do something about it; and during periods of economic ill health we have always had a considerable group which was ready to endorse positive action to end the malady. In good times little or no treatment was deemed necessary. Just as the physician, before the days of preventive medicine, assumed that he could not improve on good health, so the business man and the economist assumed that they could not improve on prosperity. In fact it was frequently supposed that if they did try to improve on it, they had an excellent chance of losing it,—of killing the goose that was currently producing all of the golden eggs.

In recent years this popular conception of an economic biology has received a severe shaking. It has become apparent that our periods of economic health pro-

*vide a standard of existence for many people far below
a level which might reasonably be expected, and it has
become evident, also, that the periods of sickness might
not only be serious, but might become chronic and lead
to complete collapse.*

*It is the aim of this book to explore further the short-
comings of the 'good health equilibrium' view of economic society in one of its sectors—that which we have
called industrial organization—and to suggest some of
the remedies or correctives which appear appropriate. In
doing this, we have sought to draw on the resources of
two rather distinct worlds. We have built the analysis
around a framework of the economic theory currently
being developed and used in the analysis of modern competitive structure, and we have sought to check this at
each turn against the experience of a business man in a
small but fairly representative section of the business
world. The reconciliation of economic theory and business experience has not everywhere been easy, but it has
been less difficult than most economists or most business
men would suppose. And while a system of economic
analysis has been the point of departure, it has not been
allowed to limit or confine the discussion. We have
dealt, also, in those less exact business observations which
have not ordinarily been incorporated in any formal
body of analysis. Hence, by the very proper criteria of
science we are ruled out from any claim to having made
a strictly scientific contribution.*

*We do not pretend for a moment that we are present-
ing a complete analysis of the weaknesses of modern
economic life. Our suggestions encompass but a small*

part of what, as we see it, must be done if modern capitalism is to have a fair chance of survival. We have said nothing at all about monetary policy, fiscal policy during depression and prosperity, taxation,[1] international trade policy, or of education and individual behavior appropriate to a workable economy. What we have attempted is an analysis and a program for one, but only one, important area of our economic life. We are as concerned with emphasizing the partial character of our effort as we are convinced of its importance within its proper limits.

We have had the counsel and support of many good friends in working out the ideas here presented. In particular, Mr. Morris E. Leeds has been intimately associated with the project from the time of its inception as part of a larger search for the ways to business progress and stability. And we have been greatly aided by the many friends who have put themselves to more than a few pains in criticizing the various working drafts through which this has passed.

While the authors have discussed vigorously all parts of the book, and each has modified his views more than he could now recall (or safely admit), yet by the nature of the case responsibility for the correctness of the theory and analysis must rest primarily upon the economist and for suggested action primarily upon the business man.

H.S.D.

J.K.G.

1. The first three subjects are covered from a business man's point of view, in *Toward Full Employment*, a forthcoming collaboration of Morris E. Leeds, Ralph E. Flanders, Lincoln Filene, and Henry S. Dennison (McGraw-Hill, 1938).

Contents

MODERN COMPETITION
AND BUSINESS POLICY

MODERN COMPETITION
AND BUSINESS POLICY

CHAPTER I
Ideal Competition and the Organization
of Industry

THE *ideal* organization of industry, from a strictly economic point of view, can be described comprehensively and yet simply. It is that all labor and capital seeking employment be used to produce those goods or render those services which people most want in the amounts which are most wanted; and that all the producing units employing the capital and labor (the factories, mines, shops, and farms) operate with the maximum of efficiency. That is to say, all willing labor and useful resources should be employed, and for the labor effort expended and the capital used there should be a maximum output of desirable goods.

But for many generations this simple statement (or some refinement of it) has been regarded as more, much more, than a statement of what would be ideal in industrial organization. It has been regarded as the state of affairs which actually exists when industry is organized by competition.

The process by which competition was supposed to achieve this happy end may be outlined in a rather simple way. Many men were imagined to be present as producers and sellers of each class of goods. Each expanded his production—as any intelligent man would—up to the point where additional production would add no more to his earnings. This is merely another way of saying that all together produced all of the goods which buyers thought it worth their while to buy and consume. If buyers wanted more goods of a particular kind they would advertise their desire by their willingness to pay more money for the articles in question. The appearance in the market of more buyers or the same buyers with a greater desire for the goods would tend to exhaust the available supply and cause prices to rise. On the other hand, these high prices would make possible and profitable an increased production of the article. This production would be extended (with falling prices) up to the point where once more producers were producing just the amount that it was worth their while to produce, while buyers were buying just the amount that they considered it worth their while to buy.

At the time of an increased demand for one article there might be a lessened demand for another one. Thus buyers might shift their expenditure from cotton shirts to silk ones. To dispose of the cotton shirts the price would have to be lowered. At the lower price it would no longer be worth while to produce the same quantity and the higher cost producers would be forced out of business if the low price persisted. No doubt some manufacturers would turn directly to the production of silk shirts; and soon, again, there would be the amount of each kind of shirt produced which was worth the while of the producers to make for sale at the price which buyers considered it worth while to pay.

Labor and capital were likewise supposed to be distributed with utmost nicety under this arrangement. When demand increased in a given line it would be possible and profitable to pay higher wages to attract workers; and the favorable prices would make new investment in capital goods attractive. At the same time in an industry where demand had fallen off, workers would be released, or their wages would be reduced and they would leave to seek better wages elsewhere. New investment in plant and machinery would be checked where demand had fallen and, perhaps, some capital equipment would be actually transferred to other lines of production.

It might even be supposed (though this is not so clear) that there would be no involuntary unemployment of labor and capital equipment under this arrangement with the exception, perhaps, of skills and capital goods which were made obsolete by shifts in demand or changes in technology, or of laborers who were in the process of changing from one job to another. Capital would seek use,—and any use is presumably better than none at all,—by lowering its price. Labor would seek employment, also, by lowering its price. For some return it would be worth while to use the total supply of capital goods and funds seeking investment. At some level of wages it would be profitable to employ the total supply of labor. With the economic system functioning at capacity there would be no reason to suppose that the (real) wage level at which full employment would be attained would necessarily be a low one. But, as the older prophets of competition did not hesitate to point out, if wages did happen to be low the situation would be self-corrective. Workers would fail to reproduce or would die young.

Such is the picture of the 'ideal' system completely regulated by competition which should produce what people want in the amounts they want, as measured by their willingness to pay; and which should make use of all available labor and capital. What of its efficiency?

A strong case was made out for the efficiency of the completely competitive system. Only by greater efficiency could any producer make a better return than his competitors. Since all bought materials, paid wages, and hired capital on an open and uniform market price basis, none could pay his labor or capital less without sooner or later having it go elsewhere. No group of producers could have excess profits (more than enough to attract their best efforts), for the excess profits would stimulate increased production by each of them in order to have the largest possible volume of sales at the favorable prices, and competitors would be attracted into the industry. For somehow the excess profits were to be widely and promptly known. These two sources of increased production would speedily eliminate the excess of profits. A producer who used his labor and capital more efficiently than his fellow producers could, however, obtain an advantage. He bought and sold at the common prices, but because of his better methods he produced at lower cost and hence, his business was likely to grow. Other producers who did not find out and adopt the better methods or find better methods of their own would run the risk of being crowded out of the industry, leaving only the most efficient producing. Thus, not only was there conceived to be a struggle for efficiency, but, also, a force which tended to spread efficiency through the industry by the survival of the fittest in the struggle for competitive profits. This spreading through the industry was synonymous with passing the benefit along to the public, for it was inevitable that it would lower prices.

CHAPTER II

The Competition of the Real World

IT has been one of the most pervasive and dangerous misconceptions of our economic and political life to think that there is only one kind of competition. And for various reasons it has been supposed that this one kind of competition was of the sort described in the preceding chapter. But, obviously, this kind of competition is quite different from that which prevails in modern industry to-day. The competition of modern industry may involve a search for greater efficiency and lower costs, but, on the other hand, it may be more concerned with outmanœuvring competitors in the matter of advertising or salesmanship; or, again, it may resolve itself into a cut throat depression of wage standards, and a lengthening of hours. Modern competition may lead sometimes to output in the quantities at which costs per unit are lowest, but far more frequently it leads to nothing of the sort. Production runs during most years at levels far below the volume which would result in the lowest cost per ton of steel or per automobile or per yard of cloth even with existing equipment.

There are, in fact, very real differences between competition of the automatic and self-regulating sort sketched in Chapter I and competition of the modern industrial world. If we can properly focus on these differences we shall have some of the problems of modern industrial organization (under-capacity production, price wars and whatnot) in reasonably clear perspective.

In modern times the only major industry where competition of the self-regulating variety has prevailed at all generally was in agricultural staples, particularly before the Great War. In more recent years even agriculture has been subject to a variety of interferences and controls some of them forced by the very fact that farmers must sell in a market made by capacity production, and buy in a market of quite another sort,—the complex-market which actually exists in the industrial world. But we can uncover many of the differences between ideal or pure competition and that which actually exists in the industrial world by contrasting the price and production behavior of the agricultural producer (under pre-war conditions) with the price and production behavior of the firm in non-agricultural production.

The relation of the individual wheat or cattle producer to price is simple:—price is something which is entirely beyond his jurisdiction or control. He plans his operations with full realization that any decrease or increase in his production will affect his selling price not at all. With the same land and capital resources as his neighbors it is only by better organization and by a more effective gauging of the expenditures which it is just worth his while to make that he can make more money than they. There is no advantage to the farmer in entering upon price competition with his neighbor, either by cutting his price, or giving secret rebates, or spending heavily for sales promotion. On the other hand he can do nothing by himself to increase the price. He may at times decide to limit production by using only part of his acreage, but he knows his restriction of production will not of itself raise the price. He will restrict only when he figures that his out of pocket costs cannot be met by the price. For the most part he will make full use of his plant and the price he gets will reflect a complex of natural and national influences over the world, all completely beyond his power to alter to any measurable extent.

Unlike the situation in agriculture, the modern organization of industry places squarely on the shoulders of the business man a measure of jurisdiction over the price of his products. This comes about from a variety of causes, of which the two most important are the presence in each market of a relatively small number of relatively large producers, and the tendency of many individual producers to acquire more or less distinct submarkets of their own.

We must pause here to warn the reader that special difficulties are encountered in the use of the adjective 'large' in economic analysis. 'Largeness' measured in terms of assets or number of employees is not very useful. A firm with assets of $10,000,000 would be large in industries manufacturing shoes or whips or sealing wax. In the steel industry or automobile industry such a firm would be all but lost from sight. To meet these difficulties we shall give 'large' and 'small' special meanings; we shall speak of firms as large or small in terms of the fraction they produce of the total output of the industries with which they operate in the same market. Thus the nation's largest wheat producer, who, however, produces an almost infinitesimal per cent of the nation's (or world's) supply of the cereal will be small in our definition. On the other hand, a $25,000 concern which produces five per cent of the country's supply of glass inkwells we shall consider large.

We can best show the difference between price behavior when there are small producers and when there are a few producers each large relative to the total market, by seeing what happens when the first situation transforms itself into the second—what happens, in other words, when many small producers become a few large ones. It is necessary to resort to a hypothetical case to illustrate the point.

The individual cattle producer as we know him must take his price for granted. His output is so small a fraction of the total that a hundred per cent increase or decrease in his supply changes prices not a whit. But let us suppose that our cattle producer (perhaps behind a substantial tariff wall) begins to grow very large and a few of his fellow-producers begin to grow likewise. Eventually he comes to produce a substantial fraction of the total output of the industry; with his far-flung range interests in his Iowa feeder subsidiary, let us say, he brings to market a quarter of the cattle of the country. His half-dozen leading competitors account together for an additional fifty per cent and a few score others for the remaining quarter. By industrial standards, it may be noted, this would be a moderate 'concentration' of the industry.

What now of our cattle producer's behavior in the

matter of price? Some time during the expansion of his enterprise he has made an important discovery—it is a discovery of something, however, which nearly every business man now takes for granted. Our cattle man has found at some stage in his growth that he cannot expand his production (other than by absorbing his competitors) and continue to neglect the effect *of his own individual expansion* on the price of cattle. At some stage in his growth he discovers that a twenty per cent increase in production which is perfectly justified by range facilities and breeding stock will depress prices to the point where his net profit is no greater or is less, perhaps, than before. He has reached the point when he must plan his production with consideration to the effect of production on price; he has accepted, whether he likes it or not, a measure of jurisdiction over price.

At this point he will find himself, necessarily, considering what price he should have for his cattle. His larger competitors will likewise soon come to decide such schedules of desirable prices for themselves. Our cattleman then lets as many cattle come off the range and pass through the feedlots as can be sold at his price. If demand falls off, fewer cattle are shipped to his Iowa feeder subsidiary; some of the feeder hands are laid off. Fewer heifers are kept for breeding so that range stocks will not become top heavy. The price remains close to where it was. It is not unlikely that by this time the cattle baron employs a corps of salesmen to solicit orders. No doubt he engages in competitive advertising, also, and worries about the 'smaller fry' in the industry who undercut his prices on branded beef.

Price decreases become a serious and difficult matter for there are the regular wholesaling and retailing customers who have stocks at existing prices to be considered, and it is possible that his competitors will not 'play ball' if it is a price increase which is in order. The trappings of modern industrial competition,—all quite foreign to the cattle producing industry as we now know it,—are complete.

We say competition deliberately, for as producer's price jurisdiction emerges, competition does not disappear; it merely changes to another of the several forms which competition may take, and it may be very keen. No one would argue, for example, that competition is absent or especially mild in the automobile industry, although the structure of the industry requires the auto manufacturer himself to decide upon a price for his own product and to produce at the scale where (considering his competitors' probable actions) he thinks net profit per car times the total output is likely to be greatest,—which only by accident will be at the scale where cost per car is lowest. For the moment, however, we are less concerned with where he fixes the price than with the simple and obvious fact that he must fix it and so must assume a measure of jurisdiction over the market price.

With some variations the sort of producer jurisdiction over price which is to be found in the automobile industry, and which we have imagined for the cattle industry, holds over the great range of American industry. The reason that the wheat producer did not take into consideration the effect of his own production on price was that his output, however 'large,' was still far too small in relation to total production to have a bearing on the price of wheat. On the other hand, where the output of a producer is large enough to have a bearing on the price of the product some measure of individual producer price influence must exist. In most lines of American industry there are several producing firms large enough to have changes in their output affect prices; no one of these firms could expect (when demand is stable) to increase its share of the total production without making a definite decision to lower its prices. This is what is meant by saying that the firm has a measure of jurisdiction over price.

CHAPTER III

The Scope of Producer Price Jurisdiction

To appreciate how widely prevalent throughout industry is the larger sized unit which makes price jurisdiction necessary, we may refer to the calculations of Berle and Means.[1] According to their estimates about one-half of the corporate assets at the beginning of 1930, and over one-third of the business wealth of the United States was controlled by the 200 largest non-banking corporations. In the case of railroads, light and power utilities, and communications companies, which are included among the 200, jurisdiction over the price of the product or service by the companies under governmental regulating bodies is, of course, complete. Of the industrial firms in this list each must be, as a simple matter of arithmetic, an important factor in its industry or industries. Each must necessarily behave as does the automobile producer,—that is, it must decide on a scale of prices and produce the quantity it can sell at those prices. In no case can it profitably follow the practice of the wheat farmer and aim to produce the quantity which would give the lowest cost without regard to the price at which that quantity can be sold.

The known importance of the mammoth concern in

1. *The Modern Corporation and Private Property*, The Macmillan Co., New York, 1933.

modern industry, and the influence it necessarily has on prices, would be sufficient to establish our case that the ideal of a pure market price and self-regulative competition is seldom realized; but price jurisdiction is by no means limited to the corporation with assets in the 50 or 100 million dollar class. Most of the industrial corporations listed by Berle and Means are large units in important national industries, such as steel, automobile, copper, aluminum, oil and chemicals. A smaller unit in a less important industry, or a small unit in a large industry like cement which is regionalized by the cost of transportation, must accept the same jurisdiction over price. In many industries action by the smallest unit with respect to its rate of production or its price scale has a measurable effect on the market.

Except in the case of automobiles we have so far been speaking of products which are standardized,—products which vary little from one manufacturer to another. Over a great range of products and services, however, there is a certain amount of differentiation between the output of one producer and another. Where this is the case there are further influences which lead to producer price jurisdiction. The wheat of any typical grower of No. 1 hard winter differs in no perceptible degree from that of a hundred or a thousand other growers. In planning his production the grower does not need to concern himself with the possibilities for increased sale of his own private brand of wheat. This is not true of the producers of branded products such as toothpaste, cosmetics, or even shoes and ready-to-wear clothing. The manufacturer of cosmetics is doubtless interested in the general market for cosmetics; in common with the rest of the trade he would like to see as many fathoms of make-up covering over as many square miles of faces as possible. But he must be still more interested in the market for his own particular brands of face powder and skin lotion. His own market may show a behavior quite different from that of the market for cosmetics in general; and within this market he is the sole seller. No person can enter with the same product, bearing the same brand name and undercut him. His prices, of course, must be within some range of relationship to those of his competitors, but within that range he must accept a fairly complete jurisdiction over them.

If we look at the matter from a slightly different point of view we may regard the producer of a branded product as having a 'monopoly' of the particular brand which he sells. The perfection of the monopoly depends on the degree in which the branded product differs from competing brands, or (what amounts to the same thing) the degree in which buyers think that it differs. The seller of the brand has a jurisdiction over the price of his product that is the same in kind, if different in degree, as that which has long been associated with monopoly. Economists have, in fact, come to refer to this form of industrial organization as monopolistic competition. The term suggests the situation to which it applies, namely a degree of jurisdiction or control over price in combination with a very real desire to compete for sales. Monopoly is not the antithesis of competition; the two can and do exist side by side, and both may be present in the transactions of a single company.[1]

Jurisdiction over price which accompanies the separation or differentiation of each producer's product or service from the others in the market is common throughout consumers goods industries and in services of all kinds, although the range of price over which the jurisdiction is effective naturally varies widely. Frequently some physical difference distinguishes the product of one producer from that of others; or the belief that there is a difference may be built up in the minds of consumers by advertising. Again, it may be a matter of habit for buyers to inquire for a given product; to patronize a certain barber; to ask for a certain camera film by its maker's name; or to resort to a given store. Wherever there is such a group of dependable customers the seller is partly protected against the undercutting of others. He may not be able to do as he likes with his prices, but on the other hand he is no longer subject to all the ups and downs of a wheat market.

There is usually a measure of producer price jurisdiction, also, where production is to order. In much production to the buyer's specification, custom and habit play a considerable part; 'shopping around,' except in some cases where bids are submitted, is difficult, and comparisons of the products and dependability of different sellers is not easy. These limitations give the seller a range in which he has jurisdiction over price. Where specialization and custom have given a certain

1. This discussion draws heavily from E.H.Chamberlin. *The Theory of Monopolistic Competition*. Harvard University Press 1933.

firm a particular line of goods,— such as a special sort of shoe box—that firm has, of course, the price jurisdiction which grows out of a small element of monopoly control.

Finally, not only do sellers have price jurisdiction, but in recent years we have seen developing in some cases a measure of price jurisdiction by buyers. In most markets the buyers are more numerous than the sellers; two decades or more ago the individual buyer of grocery products, for example, was unable, except in rare instances, to do more than 'buy at the market' in precisely the same way that the farmer sells at the market. The 'mass buyer,' however, has become increasingly important. He has the power through withdrawal or shifts of his patronage to exercise a vigorous influence on price,—or at least on the price at which *he* buys. Of the importance of the mass buyer and his effect on prices we have much yet to learn. It is apparent, however, that he is able to exercise a degree of jurisdiction over price where it was once assumed that as individuals neither buyers nor sellers could do anything but accept the dictation of the market.

It is the major contention of this book that the form of competition which involves some degree of jurisdiction over price by sellers (or buyers) exists very widely; and that the business world therefore lacks the self-regulating character which is present when competition involves no such jurisdiction. This lack of self-regulation will become apparent when, in the next chapter, we turn to consider some of the more direct consequences of producer price jurisdiction. Before going on to this, however, let us make certain that we are likely to do so in a proper frame of mind.

There is nothing about jurisdiction or control over prices which places the modern producer in a culpable or blameworthy position. It is simply one of the facts of modern industrial organization. It is not a recent change from older forms of price making, but something which has characterized most of our more modern industries since their birth. The production of automobiles, steel, petroleum products, and a host of other goods has involved a measure of producer price jurisdiction from the beginning. The situation may be good or bad, but we shall accomplish nothing unless we approach it as something into which the individual business man was born and to which he is largely or wholly subject.

CHAPTER IV

The Effects of Producer Price Jurisdiction

WE may repeat once more that under the type of competition which existed for pre-War agriculture no one controlled wheat or cotton or cattle prices. This, to a considerable extent, is still true of agriculture. In other lines of endeavor, if common observation and statistics of industrial concentration may be trusted, some degree of jurisdiction over price by producers is all but universal. The next stage of our inquiry concerns the effect of this price jurisdiction, or, more correctly, the effect of a situation which necessitates such jurisdiction.

We shall begin with the proposition that when the individual producer can influence price, the self-regulating character of competition, by this very process itself, is impaired or eliminated. When price is beyond the control of the producer, as in agriculture generally, it is an objective specification indicating the amount which society regards as the optimum to be produced. That is to say, the production which is the most profitable for the producer at that price is the amount society desires from him. But if the producer has the power to alter price, then the specification is no longer set by society, but by himself. Quite naturally he forms his price policy with his own interest in mind; it is an accident if the social and the individual interest coincide.

As it actually works out there are very good reasons why the most desirable price for the individual will be different from that which is socially most beneficial. It is to these discrepancies between the individual and the social interest that we must now turn.

Below Optimum Production: Above Optimum Price

The profitability of restricted production has long been recognized in the case of monopoly; but it is of the greatest importance that we recognize that wherever there is individual jurisdiction over prices there is the *same* incentive as there is under monopoly to produce less than the socially desirable optimum.

The extent to which it will be possible so to maintain the prices which restrict production depends on many factors, and the actual processes by which prices are supported are frequently so clouded over by other considerations or develop so gradually that they may be completely overlooked. Essentially the situation is this— one firm, in complete control of an industry, can reap additional returns by pricing above the 'pure competition' level and therefore it produces less than the amount which would be bought were prices at the 'pure competitive' level. Several firms, each doing the same thing, can jointly reap additional returns over the pure competitive level of prices and production. As has sometimes happened in the past, they may be stimulated to get together to effect a control, but more often there is a tacit acceptance of the situation and a tacit and frequently unrecognized concurrence in a policy that effects the desired goal,—a policy which reflects good business management for each concern from the point of view of its own earnings. Every individual firm whose prices are at the level where the quantity sold times net margin is maximum knows that if it cuts prices to increase its output other firms will do likewise; it knows that after the price is cut, while each may have more business as the result of the lower price, each will have lower net returns because of the lower price. It is only a matter of common intelligence to refrain from lowering prices. Nevertheless, to refrain is to prevent production from reaching the socially optimum level where labor and capital are employed up to the volume of output where per unit costs are lowest.

There are, of course, instances where a comparatively small number of large producers appear to use their individual jurisdiction over prices to support them scarcely at all,—the rubber tire industry before 1936 appears to have been an example. A single major producer who chooses to sell his product at a low price is usually able to make other producers behave in similar fashion. But the cases where some support is given to prices are far more common.

The foregoing is not an exercise in theoretical analysis; it is subject to verification at every hand. It is a commonplace that many of our industries operate for long periods at considerably below the output which would mean minimum costs for each article produced. It is a commonplace, also, that their prices have often remained comparatively stable at such times. This combination of circumstances,—which was familiar in pre-

depression as well as depression years,—means simply
that price cutting has been avoided and that production
has been below the socially desirable amount. At the
same time, net profits presumably have been greater or
net losses less than they would have been at the socially
optimum output.

We speak of losses deliberately for it is sometimes
assumed that so long as profits are moderate the industry
is operating in the public interest. This ill-conceived
supposition that if profits are low all is well with an
industry should be abandoned once and for all. As every
business man knows, earnings depend on the general
state of demand and on efficiency, and not alone upon
the price and production policy adopted. A grasp-
ing monopoly can lose money if it is highly inefficient; so can a monopoly whose goods are going out of
use. Earnings are a criterion of many things and the
single criterion of low profits cannot be used to determine the degree to which public interest is served.

Besides tacit acceptance of a given price situation
there are other ways in which production may come
to be stabilized below the optimum output. Much,—
probably too much,—has been made of agreements or
undertakings between firms. Agreements which are not
enforceable at law are of relatively little effect except
where the surrounding circumstances are highly favorable; and in such circumstances formal agreements are
hardly necessary. Firms, for example, may follow the
price and production advice of their trade association.
More common, perhaps, is the tendency to follow the
lead of some well established member of the industry.

Price leadership, so-called, has existed or is presumed to exist in the steel, petroleum, agricultural implements, anthracite, metal can, corn products, industrial alcohol, cement, and a number of other industries. In each of these industries one firm or a group of dominant firms set for themselves certain prices to which their competitors tend (or have tended) to conform.[1] The same method is followed in many less important industries, where the concerns which are unable or unwilling to figure costs adopt the price list of some leader as it stands or at such uniform discount as they think will get orders for them.

There is no question of reproach in any of this discussion of below optimum production. The individual business man in supporting prices at the expense of production is but following the course that must be taken by any intelligent man in pursuit of his own interests, or the interests of the stockholders to whom he is legally accountable. What does concern us is that aside from extreme business fluctuations (which may be a somewhat related matter as we shall see) we have in price jurisdiction and the attendant curb on potential output one significant explanation of the failure of the American economy to achieve the standards of abundance which all with a gleam of imagination know are possible.

It is already apparent that the legislation encompassed in the Sherman and Clayton Acts, and the so-called anti-trust policy, touches only an insignificant part of the problem with which we are con-

1. Cf: Arthur R. Burns, *The Decline of Competition*, 1936. Pp. 76-140.

cerned. It deals with monopolies and the monopolies which come within the definition of the Supreme Court are of very narrow importance; their restraint on the country's whole production of wealth is fractional in comparison with the perfectly legal restraints which business judgment imposes on the producer who has reached the size where he must plan his production with regard for its effect upon price. Even when the courts succeed in dissolving a 'trust' at best they only replace monopoly restraint with that dictated by business judgment, without being able to give any assurance that the prices under the latter will be lower than the monopoly price.

Price Wars and Cut-throat Competition

Perhaps the most important single incentive to the search for a new basis of industrial organization has been the experience of modern industry with what it calls cut-throat competition. N.R.A. code-making was more concerned with the problem of 'stabilizing' competition than with any of the other code provisions with the exception of those relating to labor. It is a commonplace that the greatest attraction of N.R.A. from the point of view of the business man was the prospect it held for escape from 'destructive' competition.

It may seem a paradox that over-intense price competition should be characteristic of a form of industrial organization which gives producers jurisdiction over prices. But the reasons are comparatively simple. If the producer has no power to maintain prices he has no incentive to cut them; why should he do so when the outstanding fact of his situation is that his entire production is relatively so small that it all can be sold at the going market price? But if industry has passed on to the stage where prices are supported by the individual judgment of the various competitors, the possibility of price cutting and of price wars does arise. The very fact that competitors are supporting prices means that production is below the lowest cost volume. Any one competitor may at any time plan to expand his production and bring his own plant closer to the socially optimum production. He will try this by slashing his prices, but his competitors are likely to meet his cuts and go further. If they do the fight is on.

Overhead costs enter as a vital and complicating factor in the modern price war. Reference to modern industry as 'capitalistic' means, among other things that it relies heavily on capital goods in its production processes. Plant and machinery have become increasingly important in the manufacture of commodities while the use of labor relative to capital has been diminishing. It is one of the important economic differences between a man and a factory or a machine that the man must be paid weekly for his labor while the factory or machine need be paid but once in several years or, perhaps, may never be paid at all.

The effect of all this is to lessen the importance of total costs as a floor to price movements. If labor costs are a large percentage of the final cost of manufacture, the weekly or monthly payroll will at some point force a price increase or force some producer out of business, but there is no payroll for plant and machinery.

If overhead charges bulk large in the total cost there is nothing to prevent long continued sales at prices insufficient to cover such costs,—at prices little if any above the immediate out-of-pocket costs. The producer may 'fail,' but in an overwhelming majority of cases that only means that the firm and the machines go on producing under some other legal control; or by the very failure the overhead charges of the plant may be scaled down to a level where the cut prices actually appear to cover costs. In the long run such firms may disappear, but in the long run everything disappears.

During the third quarter of the nineteenth century the rate wars of the railroads became part of the American legend. These dramatic battles of the carriers in their pre-regulation days were but a forecast of what could happen elsewhere in American industry when it took on a similar competitive structure. The railroads had a capital investment charge huge in comparison with the out-of-pocket costs of moving a passenger or a ton of freight. Under such circumstances prices or rates could be cut far below the level where they bore any relation to costs,—in the heat of the battle they might even be cut to zero. Modern industry may have lost some of the spirited vindictiveness which was in evidence when the railroad barons lashed out at each other; but the organization of industry, and the importance of 'fixed overhead,' which led the railroads to do battle, have spread to other lines of industry with similar results.

The basic evil of price wars is that they are wars. Part of the world, at least, is slowly coming to understand that, in spite of temporary appearances, modern wars are a dead loss to winners, losers, and neutrals, and profit only the munitions makers. Two of the vital new features which modern conditions have brought to warfare and which help to make it now (probably) race suicide, are distinctly interesting to a study of modern price wars. First, modern war is carried on by a large and an ever increasing proportion of the citizens of the fighting nations. Second, the defeated nation is no longer completely annihilated, enslaved, or absorbed, but stands as a living, though crippled, institution, whose peoples still dwell on their lands and run their factories. From them, somehow short of slavery, the winner's winnings, if there are to be any, must be obtained; and against their eventual attempt at bitter reprisal the winner must keep himself perpetually armed.

In modern business, too, a price warfare is most likely to involve the whole of a trade; the price cutting is not confined to a city or country market-place where surpluses may exist, or even to the goods or capacity of which there may be a surplus; and in it hurt pride and a spirit of reprisal may completely swamp economic motive and economic judgment.

The second point in analogy to national warfare is, however, the more important. Price warfare doesn't destroy the least fit among the agencies of production or distribution,—it doesn't destroy any at all, but leaves plant or machinery or stores intact or but temporarily disturbed. And they are the facilities which produce or distribute, whoever may hold legal title to them as property. The most vigorous price war may have effected a few changes in title, but that is all. There is not, therefore, even a slim chance of anything like a settlement or adjustment; there may be during the war a scaring off of new participants in the business, but they may crowd in all the faster in the piping days of peace.

To appraise the social effects of price wars and cut-throat competition in more specific terms is no easy matter. From one point of view the price war is desirable in so far as it moves an industry toward the optimum volume of production. The consumer enjoys a larger volume of goods at lower prices. If it is a gasoline war he has a jaunt that he would not otherwise have taken; if it is a milk war, the housewife has some change left over at the end of the week and the children go to a matinee. Since consumers are the most numerous people we have it is easy to argue that the price war should be encouraged. But not all price-war cutting gets through to the consumer. Much of what occurs on supplies or part-manufactured goods is absorbed in profit. Manufacturers' price wars on some consumers' shelf goods do not affect the retail price, because some such goods do not respond favorably to temporary bargain sales. One cannot quarrel with price-cutting until it reaches a point where it threatens permanent and efficient production at decent wage standards. It may be added, however, that if a price has been too high for its proper purposes before the war (which is by no means always the case since wars are frequent in 'skim-milk' trades) the soundest cure for this evil is still not an 'equal and opposite' evil, but the reaching of an intermediate balance or equilibrium. When price warfare does go beyond the intermediate equilibrium we see its sinister side, a side which is suggested by the term 'cut-throat' competition frequently applied to it. The most favorable setting for cut-throat competition is the less prosperous times when a considerable number of people are unemployed. When prices are being beaten down it is part of the producer's defence to cut cost. In an industrial society where there is a body of unemployed the bargaining strength of most classes of labor is sure to be low; and there is no more certain and direct way of cutting costs than by cutting wages, and laying off men by lengthening hours. The process can be carried to indefinite lengths as we have seen demonstrated in the needle trades and other industries in recent years.

If the industry has not reached a sufficient degree of concentration to make tacit price maintenance at some level practicable, it is especially probable that some competitor will always seek to expand his output by further price and wage decreases. Others must follow suit or lose their business. Single-handed efforts to maintain prices or wages are certain to be costly and futile. The final result is likely to be almost unbelievable misery for those employed in the industry and considerable unhappiness for those who employ them.

Where we have no price jurisdiction, as in the model competitive society outlined in Chapter I, there are no price wars. But where there is a little jurisdiction, enough to permit the individual to set his prices but not to maintain them, we have an unstable and frequently dangerous situation. This stage seems to be more dangerous, indeed, than when there is a greater degree of control.

It is a nice dilemma that we face. On the one hand producer price jurisdiction keeps industry below its most fruitful level of production; the community suffers from a smaller wealth production than it has a right to expect. On the other hand, if the price maintenance is not successful it may degenerate into predatory price cutting, whose victims are the poor unfortunates who are employed in making the goods. They, moreover, are consumers themselves and their wage cuts may at any time assist in a downward spiral of lower consuming power and lower production.

OVER-INVESTMENT AND WASTEFUL SALES PROMOTION

We come now to two less malignant but yet wasteful out-growths of producers' jurisdiction over prices. One of these, like price warfare, is rather paradoxical as a companion of price jurisdiction and below par production. It is excessive investment in an industry by those connected with it.

While a firm or a group of firms may maintain prices at the expense of optimum production, it is seldom possible to prevent the entry of new concerns to share in the profits. The better the profits have been in the industry the more probable the entry of new firms. But quite as often ignorance of the true earnings situation in the industry or the tendency to follow the crowd, may cause new firms to come in when profits are negligible or absent. The increase in the number of firms tends to split up more and more the business which is available at the prices which are maintained. Presently there is an excessive volume of equipment in the industry; the utilization of plant is so low that expenses are little more than covered; and all the while consumers are paying prices higher than they need be.

A condition such as that just described frequently appears in real life in a somewhat more complicated form, but is an underlying characteristic in a number of important industries. In almost all parts of the country it is possible at a given moment to stabilize the retail price of gasoline with fair success. On the other hand it is impossible to prevent new individuals or concerns from entering the business of retailing gasoline. The filling station is a more than normally attractive field for small enterprise since it requires only a small capital outlay and comparatively little business acumen; many people have sought to escape unemployment by acquiring station sites and starting in business. The result is an investment in gasoline retailing establishments grossly in excess of need or even of convenience. For all or a large part of this the consumer pays in the price of gasoline, while at the same time little or no net return is earned by the retailers. The retailing of milk in many, perhaps most, cities has presented a roughly similar picture; and other fields of retailing show excess facilities and dilution of business to a substantial degree.

Where prices are maintained at the expense of optimum production we encounter, also, a waste in the form of excess sales promotion activity and advertising expenditure. Any firm within an industry can gain a larger and, ordinarily, a lower cost output if it gets business away from its rivals. To increase business is still more to its advantage if it can continue to sell at the same price. If, for obvious reasons, it does not wish to cut prices there are still two ways in which a firm can take business from its competitors. One is to produce a better quality of article, and the other is to spend more money on advertising and sales promotion. With quality competition society does not have much quarrel, and no one doubts that it is an important force in present day business. But advertising and sales promotion pure and simple are much more frequent devices for maintaining or increasing one's share in the market. And here the social purpose of the extra expenditure is open to question.

It has been estimated that in 1929 the cost of marketing all goods in the United States amounted to more than 24 billion dollars. For such goods as require manufacture the cost (value added by manufacture) was 28 billions. Apparently, we spend nearly as much on distribution services, and facilities, advertising and salesmen, as in our mills and factories. The costs of marketing, moreover,—judging by employment figures,—are increasing rapidly. In 1930 the number employed in manufacture had increased some 32 per cent over the number so employed in 1910. The number employed in agriculture in 1930 had changed little from 1910. In marketing, on the other hand, some 68 per cent more workers were employed in 1930 than in 1910.[1]

Much marketing expenditure is quite as necessary and useful as expenditure for manufacturing or agriculture.

1. Data from J. K. Galbraith and John D. Black. *The Quantitative Position of Marketing in the United States.* The Quarterly Journal of Economics. May, 1935.

This applies, for example, to the provision of the necessary and convenient amount of jobbing, wholesaling and retailing service. But it is plain that part of the huge expenditure on marketing services and part of the increase in recent years reflect the costs of over-investment, competitive advertising and high pressure selling effort which our analysis of modern industrial organization would lead us to expect. This part of the present marketing expenditure serves no more useful social purpose than to separate the other fellow from a part of his business. The business man and the community are heavy losers in the battle; benefit accrues only to the advertising firms and the salesmen who participate in the war or contribute munitions. Highly prized gains in manufacturing efficiency are piddled away in the cost of the selling strife.

The superficial view, of course, is that men are employed and made happy by the contest. The more searching conclusion is that they would be better employed and equally happy creating articles or services which the community needs, and with which it would be so much the richer. In any case one can scarcely countenance boondoggling in business, however happy the boondogglers may be. We might ask any housewife her preference as between advertising circulars or door-to-door canvassers and more and cheaper clothing for her family!

Finally, if there is doubt about our conclusion that excess advertising and sales promotion activity is an appendix to the price jurisdictional practices of modern industry, let us refer once more to our bench mark. We may ask any major advertising agency how many accounts, if any, it has of individual staple farmers. Or, for that matter, how much gross revenue it receives from the bituminous coal industry or the cotton piece goods trade, both of which still adhere, more or less, to their original competitive structure, and, by contrast, we may ask how much is received from the cigarette industry where producer price jurisdiction is complete. We believe the agency will agree that jurisdiction over prices though something less than a cause of advertising is a necessary condition if there is to be heavy advertising expenditure.

We do not, of course, consider all advertising wasteful. Market knowledge is improved and the consumer benefited when the wholesaler or retailer makes known the prices and qualities of his offering. New lines of goods are constantly appearing which are capable of rendering considerable satisfaction to consumers when known. Some fanfare of trumpets is necessary to make the article familiar. But not all and, perhaps, not much of the present expenditure of time and energy on advertising and sales promotion can be considered of this order.

CHAPTER V

The Problem of Adaptation in a Changeable World

THE effects of present day industrial organization outlined in the preceding chapter would hold even if we were dealing with the most settled and mature of industrial communities. If that community had the price organization which we have described, we should have to expect the below optimum production, unemployment, cut-throat competition, and the wasteful competitive investment and sales promotion which we have analysed.

Our industrial community, however, is far from settled, mature, and static. It must accommodate itself to an increasing population,—which, moreover, is prone to change its living and buying habits. Technical processes change and with them the supply and competitive position of different products and the strength and importance of competing firms. Most important of all, our industrial organization experiences booms and depressions; irregular cycles of expanding, contracting, and, again, expanding purchasing by consumers and by users of capital goods.

In a self regulating system the mechanism of primary importance in the process of adjustment to changes of a technical character, and to changes in tastes and buying habits, is price change; virtually all adjustments are expected to work themselves out by means of alterations in prices. If a combine harvester, for example, cuts the cost of producing wheat, this is assumed to lift the returns of the wheat grower above the returns of the producers of other crops on lands which could be used for wheat, and cause wheat production to increase and wheat prices to fall. The fall in prices would be expected to continue until expansion was checked and the industry once more in adjustment. The advantage of the combine harvester as against the binder and thresher would be passed along to the community at large in the form of lower prices for breadstuffs.

The process of adjustment to cyclical fluctuations also involves price changes. A boom period is a time when demand is strong, when more people are willing and able to pay more money for consumers goods. A depression is a period when demand is sharply curtailed,—when fewer people with a lessened willingness to spend are in the market to buy. Under 'pure' competition curtailment of demand means, of course, an immediate fall in prices. They must fall enough so that the market will absorb the supply currently available; so that price times quantity is equal to the amount that consumers or buyers are willing to spend. During the boom period the situation is reversed. Demand is improving; the essence of the increase is the willingness of purchasers to spend more money for goods. The process of spending more money involves bidding by buyer against buyer and an upward response in prices.

Under an ideal self-regulative system where no producer is large enough to affect price and there is an open market, these price changes would be sensitive, prompt and cover practically all goods and services. That prices in most of the industrial world have no such prompt and sensitive response is a matter of common knowledge. Just how prices of specific goods do behave has not been too thoroughly studied and recorded. From Means's work[1] it is clear that price movements vary greatly as among different types of merchandise; and that within each of his ten groupings of similar movements there are strange assortments. But a very short life in the business world is enough to convince one that few prices indeed are fluid or sensitive enough to induce prompt adaptations to the almost constant technical and cyclical changes of the modern world.

Before trying to describe in what ways prices seem to the business man to fluctuate, one factor of the price problem may be mentioned by way of parenthesis. Practically all thinking about price as an economic hormone, and virtually all information about prices assume a uniform price at any minute to all buyers of the same class. Yet all buyers and sellers in the business world know that special and secret discounts, prices and concessions exist in good times and bad. No one knows what they really amount to or how much they would make average price differ from published price; and, moreover, it is by no means certain that when an average price changes because heavy special concessions are made to 5 per cent of the buyers, the effects towards adaptation are the

1. Gardiner C. Means: *Industrial Prices and Their Relative Inflexibility*. Senate Document B, 74th Congress, 1st Session 1935.

same as if the new average price had been given to all buyers. Discussion having to do with actual price behavior must of necessity leave this factor out of account, in spite of the possibility that it may be important.

If all materials connected with agriculture are excepted, the general picture of the price history on a single item of merchandise during any but extraordinary times would to the business man's eye be step-like,—a series of landings separated from each other at capricious distances by irregular up and down steps. Some merchandise,—many tools and other instruments of production, for example,—would have few, or actually no steps over many years. And those which change more frequently he would see holding to each of its levels long after the influence towards change had set in,—until, in fact, an accumulation of pressures forced a jump, or quite often a series of jumps fairly close together. The general picture, in short, is characterized by lags and over-compensations.

Such price movements are what we should expect in a system which includes producers who have to decide upon the prices at which they will sell. When a depression starts, a certain amount of salesmen's cutting or splitting commissions with favored customers may begin fairly soon, but before a general price adjustment can be made some person or committee or board of directors must take a decision. They must consider whether the fall in demand is to be of a serious and extended sort and what actions competitors are likely to take; for a cut is easy to make though usually hard to hold in control, and the corresponding raise which must be anticipated is always difficult to make and may drag months beyond the day of recovery. All these considerations take time,—often several months. In the most favorable cases 'administered-price' changes will lag well behind the situations they are assumed to meet.

In many lines of goods there are additional difficulties which face the seller in any decision to change price. Often the first cuts after a more or less extended period of price stability must be expected to reduce purchasing heavily, since buyers usually suppose that a first cut will induce a second, and will not be averse to 'turning on heat.' This upside-down phenomenon (technically, a positively inclined demand curve) is common in the business world with all sorts of buyers through to the consumer. It occurs both as a spurt in buying on price increases and as a check in buying on decreases, and depends, of course, upon the existence of a cushion of inventory or contracts. This cushion may take care of anywhere from two to four months of non-buying and a similar period of overbuying. Where, moreover, there is a chain of commission merchants, wholesalers and retailers between factory and consumer, which is true of a large proportion of consumers goods, another factor enters into a manufacturer's decision to reduce price. He must, if he is to lead a reduction, be ready to face the cost in money or good will of the loss to dealers on their inventories. Or if the situation is such that dealers believe they can sell their stocks before reducing their prices, a very serious lag may occur between the situation which calls for a price reduction and the actual reduction to the ultimate consumer where it can move goods into consumption.

Price adaptation is seriously hindered, also, by the tendency of prices to become habitual or customary, or to find levels from which they cannot move except by a jump to another level. Goods come to be classed as three dollar lines, two-fifty lines, and dollar lines, or, again, as twenty-five cent lines, fifteen cent lines, and ten cent lines. The reduction of a three dollar line may result only in its being confused by consumers with a lower quality line of goods. To reduce a fifteen cent line at all frequently means that it must be reduced to ten cents,—a reduction of one-third. There is naturally a hesitation to break down any established schedule of prices. Where the consumer is likely to misinterpret the new price, or where the drop or raise must be extreme, the hesitation is even greater. Prices are, therefore, maintained until the downward or upward pressure can no longer be withstood; then it is probable that the change will be sudden and considerable.

It is particularly difficult for the manufacturer to make price adjustments if there is resistance to 'in-between' retail prices, for example, to prices between 10 and 15 cents. The manufacturers' selling price cannot usually be above 6 cents for a retail price of 10 cents; or above 9 cents for a retail price of 15 cents. For retail prices to be cut from 15 cents to 10 cents means for the manufacturer a 33⅓ per cent reduction, i.e., from 9 to 6 cents. If costs are more than 6 cents and unlikely to drop with any increase in sales then the reduction is out of the question. If, however, costs are 5 cents the practical question which the manufacturer must answer, when considering a reduction of retail prices from 15 cents to 10 cents, is whether the increase in sales will be enough to make his new 1 cent margin yield as much as his present 4 cent margin does. Even if he could count on doubling quantity at 10 cents he would have to see a cost reduction of 1 cent or 20 per cent. Neither the doubling of quantity nor the 20 per cent reduction in cost is likely to be considered very probable. Such being the case he is likely to let prices stay where they are if it is within his jurisdiction to do so.

If the industry is one which undertakes resale price maintenance, or has habitual or widely advertised prices, price changes involve complicated problems of dealer and retailer relations. Or if a manufacturer outside the field of retailed items has a large number of lines, then new price lists and discount calculations must be made and salesmen trained to use them. There is a large degree of pure inertia to be overcome. A given price schedule may come to be taken for granted just as the brass name plate on the office building is taken for granted. Prices become customary or 'institutionalized.'

In the important field of capital goods,—those goods which get their value from their help in producing other goods which people want,—we find price behavior so stodgy that 'price rigidity' is taken for granted. When capital goods are not wanted because surplus equipment already exists to fill demand,—they are just not wanted. No 'adjusting' price decrease will sell a dollar's worth more; during depression, cuts of 50% and 75% in second hand machinery, for example, may arouse only a mild interest. Halving of the prices of automatic lathes will not stimulate sales to auto manufacturers if they are not expanding, remodelling, or renewing plant. No reduction in the price of automatic lathes is likely in itself to induce the automobile manufacturer at such times to expand or even to replace obsolete or worn-out equipment. Yet when capital goods are wanted, they are frequently wanted badly and the price is not too closely haggled over. If the firm could not fill its orders it would suffer a loss in money and prestige perhaps considerably out of proportion to the cost of the capital goods in question.

Where price inflexibility or 'rigidity' is established anywhere, it tends to spread through the system. One producer's prices are in many cases another's costs, and rigid costs reinforce the disinclination to change prices. Whenever one line of goods is used to produce another line which does not fall in price, or whenever a line is used jointly with other lines which do not fall, lower prices are not likely to result in increased sales. Lower prices for copper wire will not necessarily increase sales of wire if the wire-using industries do not reduce their prices; plumbing supply concerns will not increase their sales much by lowering prices so long as the other materials for house-building stay up. If sales cannot be increased at lower prices there is obviously no reason for the individual industry, considering its own interest, to reduce its prices. Thus price rigidity once started tends to produce a general hardening of the arteries of the economic system.

All through discussions of administered prices it is to be remembered that business men and boards of directors logically must concern themselves with net profit, i.e., the net margin per unit over unit costs, times total sales. After a voluntary decrease in price there must be a chance that the sales will increase enough to compensate for the narrow margin on each article. In 1936 the average net profit of 577 leading manufacturing corporations was 7.6 cents in each sales dollar.[1] To maintain profits with a 5 per cent reduction in price the 'average' concern would require a 200 per cent increase in sales provided costs did not change. The assumption is usually made, or implied, of course, that per unit costs go down as sales increase. This is not a dependable assumption; and the assumption that sales will increase for the industry as a whole (that demand is elastic) is by no means universally valid.

THE EFFECT OF ERRATIC ADAPTATION

Economists have still much to learn about the full effects of rigid prices and erratic price adaptation on the operation of the economy and we can here venture but a little way on the matter. But that little way is enough, for it is clear—that rigidity and erratic adaptation are serious strictures on the self-regulative features of the model competitive economy. Technological advance, for example, need not work itself out now through lower prices, enlarged consumption, and, perhaps (as many once argued) eventual increases in employment. An in-

1. National City Bank Letter. April, 1937.

vention now may mean only lower costs, larger profits and fewer workers. Or, again, adjustments to changing technology instead of proceeding *pari passu* with the changes may be resisted until the accumulated stresses produce a violent price upheaval in the industry. The result may be a period of insecurity and uncertainty for employers and employees alike. The effects of a change in demand may be similar. Price decreases may be resisted when demand falls off and this may accelerate the decrease in the volume of transactions. The adjustment when it comes is likely to be violent and, paradoxically, it may also place a temporary restraint on sales as buyers anticipate still greater bargains later on. In the opposite situation, price increases, rather than providing a gradually increasing resistance to expanding demand, may appear suddenly and in a magnitude which may first cause an added rush to buy and then later may constitute a serious check to the output of the industry.

This argument might be summarized in slightly different terms by considering for a moment the effect of such irregular price movements on the state of business certainty or uncertainty. Under the ideal state of competition which we sketched in Chapter I, there is a considerable predictability about price and production movements. Thus it is fairly certain that increased consumer demand will cause higher prices in the immediate future and that decreased demand will have the reverse effect unless indeed the cost situation in the industry happens to be changing at the same time. Similarly new inventions or other cost reductions mean larger supplies and lower prices. One can be fairly certain about such things, and given the facts can even reach some judgment on the magnitude of the expected changes.

Under the forms of competition we now know, such simple rules do not apply. The effects of changes in demand, as we have seen, may be resisted for an unpredictable period and then prices may move with quite unpredictable violence. The effects of cost changes are dependent on individual responses and are likewise unpredictable as to time and extent. The consequence of all this is that business is unpredictable and therefore uncertain and unstable. It may be convenient at times to attribute such uncertainty to 'outside' factors—to the possibility of war or to the intransigence of a President. But some day it will become difficult to overlook the fact that modern business organization is itself unstable. Aunt Sally, we all recall, was finally forced to admit that the wart was on the end of her nose and not, as she tried to suppose, on Uncle Henry's chin.

There is, moreover, the possibility that price rigidity and erratic price adaptation may have an important effect in intensifying the cycle of boom and depression. We are on dangerous ground here for most of the issues are still subjects of dispute. A model competitive system such as we outlined in the first chapter might well have a business cycle, particularly if it had banks, capital goods, and consumers durable goods and changes in the willingness of its producers and consumers to make investment or spend their income. But if, in face of the astringent influences of a period of deflation, prices declined smoothly and more or less uniformly, we may suppose that the effect on goods production and consumption would be less severe than at present. Prices rather than production, it is to be remembered, would decline in the first instance for no producer would make a single-handed attempt to stem the fall by curtailing his own output. But if the farmer, who was receiving but two-thirds as much as before for his cotton could at the same time buy his fertilizer, gasoline and clothing for two-thirds as much as before, his reduction in purchases would be comparatively mild. They would be very mild, indeed, if he had a prompt and equal reduction in freight rates, taxes, and interest. The milder the reduction in his purchases, of course, the milder the slump in industrial production, employment, and spending attributable to him. The same reasoning may be applied to other members of the industrial community.

We cannot suppose the self-regulative economy,—the model society of *laissez faire* theorists to be entirely exempt from depression-causing influences, for there would be no point in talking of smooth and uniform price declines unless there was something which curtailed spending and caused prices to fall. But it does seem clear that when we add to our model society viscous and erratic price movements, as we know them to-day, there is a greater chance that a given deflation will last longer and proceed farther than when such price behavior is ruled out. We have the stage all set for stresses and strains between different sections of the system and for sudden breaks, all of which may intensify and perpetuate a downward spiral of prices, production, and employment. We venture the opinion that the price behavior inherent in and necessary to modern industrial organization is capable of turning a mild depression into a bad one or of making a bad one into a worse.

CHAPTER VI

The Unit in Modern Industrial Organization: The Problems of the Present Day Corporation

THE phrase 'industrial organization' as we use it, refers to such degrees of co-ordination of the more or less independent activities of all of the various firms and individuals comprising our industrial society as will cause them to function more nearly for the general welfare. In our economic system such co-ordination as we have had has been worked out largely through the price machinery. Up to this point it is upon competition and price that we have centred our attention.

There are problems, also, which concern the units directly responsible for the production of goods and services,—the units which are co-ordinated as distinct from the processes of co-ordination. Our task of analysis here, however, is a simpler one than in the case of organization at large. The changes which have occurred in competition and price making have been gradual and subtle.[1] That they are still unrecognized is witnessed by the number of business men, journalists and even economists who talk of the self regulating character of com-

---

1. In many cases they have not been changes at all. The power to influence and in some measure to control prices as elsewhere described, may have developed more or less simultaneously with the development of the industry. This is true in the case of automobiles, steel, aluminum, and a host of other products.

petitive enterprise. On the other hand, the changes in the units, which, as we shall see, are mainly changes in the size and structure of the corporation, are open and obvious. In many cases it is only their relation to the public welfare which has not been thoroughly publicized.

The most important, in many respects the all important structural change in the business unit during the last century has been the change from the private or proprietary business or partnership to the corporation. Before 1800 only some 300 business corporations had been chartered in the United States. Most of these were for the construction and operation of transportation facilities or for banking and insurance. Virtually no manufacturing was carried on by corporations.[1] In 1929 there were over 300,000 corporations other than banks and financial concerns. The corporation had come to hold exclusive sway in rail transportation and communication, and it was estimated that in 1929[2] over 94 per cent of all manufacturing was done by corporations. The corporation is somewhat less important in the construction industry and in mercantile enterprise, but clearly is gaining ground. Agriculture is the only major industry where the corporation remains unimportant.

No less striking than the spread of corporate enterprise has been the increase in the size of individual units. At the beginning of 1930 the 200 largest corporations were estimated to control roughly one-half of the

1. J.S.Davis. *Essays in the Earlier History of American Corporations*. Harvard University Press.
2. Berle and Means. Op. cit. p.27. See also 'Big Business: Its Growth and Place.' Twentieth Century Fund. 1937.

corporate assets of the country. From one-sixth to one-quarter of the total national wealth was controlled by these 200 concerns, the gross assets of which ranged from 100 million dollars to 4228 million.[1]

It is important, in viewing this remarkable growth of corporate enterprise, for us to remember that the corporation is peculiarly the off-spring or creation of the state. It depends for its initial existence on the state, and without the state to recognize and protect it, it could not last for a week. The corporation is, perhaps, the outstanding example of government interference with private business. For several centuries governments were exceedingly chary in the grant of power to individuals to create a synthetic personality for the express purpose of conducting business. By the same token they were slow in accepting the responsibility for protecting this synthetic creation. If there had not been a change in the attitude of the state on these matters within the last hundred years private business would have remained exceedingly private indeed.

Two sorts of problems have been spawned by the present day corporate structure of business and for our purposes it is necessary to draw a line between them. On the one hand we have problems of the corporation which are problems because they are related to the functioning of the economic system. On the other hand we have problems of the corporation which are problems because our sense of what is moral and just in busi-

1. Berle and Means. P.95-115. The Twentieth Century Fund, basing its estimates on different and in some ways less comprehensive sources, arrives at a somewhat smaller figure for the concentration of corporate wealth.

ness relations is involved. A question concerning the effectiveness of management in the modern corporation obviously falls in the first class; for ineffective management means inefficiency, and the general public suffers through having a smaller output of goods than it might have at higher cost than there is need to pay. The second class of problems runs the gamut of fake and questionable stock promotion, 'thimble-rigging' by insiders, stock manipulation, and so forth. These are problems of business law and ethics and of equity as between individuals. Too sharp a line cannot be drawn between the two classes of problems, for the second class must unquestionably have a long run bearing on the effectiveness of the corporation as an instrument for promoting economic welfare. But it is the first class of problems, those concerning the economic functionings of the corporation, with which we are concerned. We seek to look at the particular places where the corporation, as the dominant unit in modern economic life, conflicts with or fails to advance the economic interests of the community at large.

CONTROL WITHOUT OWNERSHIP: OWNERSHIP WITHOUT CONTROL

The development of the corporation has involved an almost continuous delegation of power by the stockholder owners. At an early stage in England before the joint stock company ceased to be a loose association of semi-independent merchants, delegation of power began. No considerable number of scattered and unprofessional stockholders could provide decisive and technically competent management. Decisiveness could be obtained by delegating authority to a directorate; technical competence could be obtained by the directorate delegating management and, also, some policy decisions to a professional manager. As soon as a corporation directorate is elected there is some loss of control by the ownership interest. This would be true even where there is complete unanimity in the selection of the directorate; where there is a minority interest without representation on the board there exists some ownership with no control. Even if the minority is represented on the board its actual control may be slight.

The *rationale* of such separation of ownership from control as occurs with the traditional majority-controlled corporation is familiar, of course. Both majority and minority are regarded as being concerned with having the earnings of the company at a maximum. Differences between the majority and minority can only be differences of opinion as to how this end may be achieved. It is quite proper that those with the largest amount at stake should have the right to determine policies of the corporation.

This simple conception, like many of the others upon which our economic system was originally built, is now quite out of date. Many of our corporations are still governed in accordance with the majority principle, and policies and decisions reflect the will of the majority ownership interest. In the case of the corporations which actually count,—those which are responsible for the great bulk of the nation's transportation and communication, or its factory and power output,—control no longer rests even with the majority of the stockholders.[1]

The processes by which the great majority of stock-holders have become separated from control in the modern corporation are so varied that no detailed dis-cussion of them can be attempted here. Certainly, the most significant factor is the sheer size of the modern corporation and the wide diffusion of the ownership of its stock. When the individual stockholder joined with the majority to delegate authority to a board of direc-tors he still retained the power to join with other owners to expel his stewards if their stewardship was not to his liking. In the modern corporation even this power of selection and expulsion of the directorate is gone, or all but gone so far as the great majority of the ownership is concerned. The individual stockholder does not know the merits of those who contend for the control of the directorate; he has little or none of the materials which might enable him to judge by results. Earnings may be good or bad because of the competence or incompetence of the officers; but they may be good or bad, also, be-cause of the good or bad condition of business in gen-eral. With the most complete information it would be difficult for the stockholder to distinguish one set of causes from another, and the modern corporation 'in the interests of the company,' and in order to keep it out of the hands of competitors withholds much of the in-

1. In 1929 only 22 of the 200 largest non-banking corporations were controlled by private ownership of all the common stock or by the owners of a majority stock interest. These 22 cor-porations had 8 billions in assets which may be compared with the 76 billions of assets of the remaining 178 companies that were controlled by owners of less than a majority of the stock. Data from: *Berle and Means*, op. cit., p.27.

formation which would be absolutely essential for such a judgment.

We shall later present a case, based on grounds of general or social advantage, for rather complete information about the affairs of our corporations. But the best of information would not much alter the position of the stockholder. Unless he owns a substantial proportion of the total stock his power to act on the basis of such information is all but nil. Before he can hope to do anything it is necessary to convince other stockholders of the validity and sincerity of his own position. This he must do at his own expense; the management can do battle against him at the expense of the company. The battle is likely to be more expensive than could be compensated by any increase of the earnings or the value of his stock, and there is little likelihood that it will be successful. All the while the stockholder has a simple and convenient alternative. He can sell the stock, shouldering his loss, if any. Stockholder revolts are not unknown, but it is little wonder that they are headlined on the financial pages when they do occur, and it is worth noting, also, that these occasional revolts are almost always led by some important stockholder interest; an uprising of small rank-and-file stockholders is almost unknown.

Separation of the ownership from the control in the modern corporation comes about as the corporation increases in size, and stock ownership becomes more diffused, however straightforward and simple the capital structure and however rigorous the corporation laws. In actual practice capital structures are not simple and corporation laws are not scrupulously designed to prevent control from being lodged in the hands of a limited proportion of the ownership interest. There are a number of special devices which aid in separating control from ownership. The voting trust, non-voting stock, stock with unequal voting rights, and most spectacular of all, the holding company, are designed to further the same end. During the 1920's the Van Sweringens controlled the Hocking Valley Railroad, a subsidiary of Chesapeake and Ohio with a total ownership interest of one-quarter of one per cent of the outstanding common stock. Their ownership in the Chesapeake and Ohio, an important property, was reduced with the aid of four holding companies to less than one per cent. The remaining ninety-nine per cent of the ownership interest was without voice in the control. The Erie railroad, a half billion dollar company, was controlled through five holding companies, and the Chesapeake and Ohio by an ownership interest which amounted to six tenths of one per cent.[1]

The above are extreme, but by no means exceptional cases of control by a fractional ownership interest. One hundred and thirty of the 200 corporations investigated by Berle and Means were controlled by a directorate which was made secure in its position by widely scattered stock ownership, or which had achieved the same end by pyramiding holding companies, by the use of non-voting stock, or some other legal device. In the case of all 130 of these companies stock ownership by

[1] Berle and Means. P.74. Based on *Regulation of Stock Ownership in the Railroads*. House Reports No.2789, 71st Congress, 3rd Session.

the control was a small fraction (apparently often less than five and rarely as much as ten per cent) of the total.[1]

Where stock ownership is widely dispersed, the *de facto* control of the modern corporation rests partly with the operating heads of the business and partly with a banker or investment house group or groups. The banker makes his initial appearance to represent the corporation's financial backing and source of credit or appears at the insistence of the issuing house which has floated the corporation's securities.

In the control of the modern large corporation directors are thus in reality cast in a fiduciary role. It is important to notice, however, that they are under none of the legal restrictions and limitations which have long been considered necessary where the trustee or fiduciary was openly and bluntly recognized as such.

THE CONSEQUENCES OF THE SEPARATION OF OWNERSHIP FROM CONTROL

We do not propose to join in the weeping and wailing over the uninformed and helpless stockholder. A substantial fraction of total stock ownership at any time is in the hands of people who care not the least about the control of the corporations in which they own stock. They care little, in any immediate sense, about earnings.

1. In general, corporations were classified as management controlled if five per cent or less of the stock was held by the dominant stockholder interest. Fifty-eight per cent of the assets of the 200 largest corporations were owned by management controlled corporations as thus defined. Ibid. Pp.93-94. Cf. also page 68.

The stock was bought on the hope that it would rise in value; interest in the corporation begins and ends with the daily market quotations or with selections in the form sheets of investment services. A dividend is only one of the features of a stock which affect its market quotations.

But there is another and broader question which does concern us here. It has been supposed by many generations of economists and taken for granted by many generations of business men, that the search for individual profit is the leading stimulus to the human energy, both mental and physical, which does the world's business. It is regarded as the power which builds ships and factories and causes men to man and run them. The search for individual profit is expected to drive the machinery in a forward direction from the point of view of the community and (again from the point of view of the community) at an optimum speed.

In the case of the modern business unit, the corporation, there is a major question as to whether the individual profit motive is so geared to the drive-shaft that all the power is exerted in a forward direction. The wider the separation between ownership and control and the smaller, relative to the total, the stockholdings of the control become, the more this doubt arises. As the proportion of the stock held by the control diminishes it shares a smaller proportion of any diminution of the earnings of the corporation. On the other hand, there exist a variety of methods by which the control can gain at the expense of net earnings. The most direct of these methods is in the matter of salaries and bonuses. Salaries of corporation officials have become a matter of considerable public interest and investigation in recent years. To the unemotional student of recent corporate development this should not be a matter for surprise. The choice in the distribution of corporate earnings lies in some part between distribution as dividends and distribution as remuneration to the officers of the corporation. In the original design of the corporation this choice was to be made by the stockholders. In the typical larger modern corporations the decision between dividends and remuneration is made by those who receive the remuneration or by those who have a very small percentage of the stock affected by the decision. Where control is secure and the individual profit motive rules we must expect that remuneration will take precedence over dividends.

We have used the case of salaries to show the divergence between the individual profit motive and the stockholder interest because the lines of the conflict are clear and because it has attracted attention in recent times. But the most direct avenues of gain to the control come, perhaps, through dealings in the stock of the corporation. Information affecting the value of the stock goes first to those in control. By acting on this information it is possible to levy directly against existing stockholders who sell without 'inside' knowledge or upon the public and the amateur speculators who buy without such knowledge. When control is effected by a pyramid of holding companies, the earnings of the corporation become decidedly secondary at certain times to the gains from manipulating the capital structure. Certainly the energies of those in control, in the more extreme cases at least, are largely devoted to the intricacies of their corporate grapevine. We hazard the guess that ossification of the corporate bureaucracy, favoritism, nepotism, and inadequate personnel control become more serious when the ownership interest (which pays the bill) is weak or without voice in control.

It is not necessary to the foregoing analysis that actions of the controlling interest be calculated and 'with malice aforethought.' Acting consciously against the interest of the company is not unknown in this country, but is unusual. Even where there is no evidence of conscious decisions running counter to company interest, the separation of ownership from control is certain to make hazardous any dependence upon individualistic, economic motives to drive a corporation hourly and persistently towards its own best good.

Corporation officials have been at considerable pains in recent years when faced with regulation or taxation to show that the welfare of the stockholder, and of the security holder generally, was identical with the public welfare. In the limited extent to which this is true, any divergence of interest between the corporation control and the stockholder becomes a divergence between the control and the public welfare. The public, however, has a stake in the problems we are considering which is broader than the interests of the investing group. If the corporation management drives squarely for increased earnings through increased efficiency and lower cost production, the public gains by having more goods at a lower price. If the greater reward is for skilful manipulation of salaries or of the stock of the corporation, or its capital structure, then it is here that the effort will be applied. The search for profits can no longer be depended upon to increase efficiency but instead the public supports a piece of inefficient and high cost machinery in the prices which it pays.

Let us turn to a somewhat related set of circumstances which make for a misdirection of the profit motive in modern corporate enterprise.

The Disappearance of Business Identity

There is rarely any doubt as to the boundaries of an individual's business. They are set definitely and simply by the ownership interest of the proprietor. So far as he is motivated by the desire for profits he seeks to make what he owns yield the maximum. He may share some of his control with his creditors, but they, also, are all but certain to encourage him to make his business and each part of it yield a maximum.

As soon as the corporation appears, however, we depart from this simple unit,—simple because it is always to be identified with an individual person. In place of the individual in control there is typically a group of individuals. Typically, also, some or all of these individuals have an ownership or property interest in the stock of the corporation and other property interests outside of it. As more and more property comes to be owned in corporate form, it becomes more and more certain that their outside property interests will be in other corporations. Any person remotely familiar with American corporate practice knows that we are not dealing with a hypothetical situation; on the contrary it is one which is so typical that it rarely attracts notice or comment. No longer can we identify an individual business; every business (with rare exceptions indeed) is related to other businesses through common contribution to the wealth of some individual or banking group which is interested in two or more concerns.

It is a basic assumption of our particular form of economic organization, we may repeat once more, that each individual is motivated by the search for *individual* profit. In modern society the corporation is the unit for action; the individual remains the unit for motives. But corporations do not produce separate and distinct products and each does not sell to the final consumer. On the contrary they are related to each other as buyer to seller, seller to buyer, and competitor to competitor. Wherever an important individual ownership interest bridges two corporations which do business with or against each other, the individual profit motive is an *alternative* to the interests of the corporation and the public,—individual profit is not identical with the general good. The individual's ownership in one concern can be used to influence or direct sales and purchases so that his larger interest elsewhere is benefited. Or it may be possible to get business favors or compensations elsewhere by skilful direction of intercorporate dealings.

In an interlocked corporate structure the corporation which suffers may not be the least efficient; it may be the one that is most subservient to larger stockholder interests in other concerns. On the other hand, it is apparent that a corporation can grow and be prosperous, not solely because it is efficient, but because it may have favorable connections with other concerns. As we suggested at the beginning of this chapter, we have no intention of compiling an index of the short-comings of the modern corporation or of modern corporate practice; those authors who have undertaken such a task have produced books much thicker than this one. But we are concerned with showing that well within the boundaries of legal (and even of ethical) conduct there is no assurance that modern corporate enterprise rewards socially desirable and penalizes socially undesirable behavior. On the contrary, we have seen that the separation of the control from ownership and what we have termed the loss of business identity, have led to a very different scheme of rewards. In consequence, though we might once have counted upon the profit motive as an automatic propellent toward economy and efficiency in business operations, it is now quite capable of propelling business in an entirely different direction.

CHAPTER VII
The Alternative Courses of Action

IN the preceding chapters we have looked over the regulating mechanism, or rather the lack of regulating mechanism, under modern forms of competition. It is apparent that there are many faults:—faults which stand revealed when we measure the system, not against the performance of some form of collectivist society, but against the expected or supposed achievements of a competitive society. The situation we have analysed, we may add, is integral to the present day organization of industry. It cannot be dismissed as the product of government interference, the stupidity of bankers, or the cupidity of labor leaders.

When we turn to the question of what, if anything, can be done about these weaknesses, we are faced first of all with a question of basic design. It is of considerable importance to an architect who is about to submit plans for a building that he know whether it is to be a skyscraper or a warehouse. We must know what kind of business structure we seek.

Apart from thorough-going socialization of industry, the choices in design seem to be two. On the one hand we may hope for a business organization which is self-regulating in a more or less automatic way. It happens that the only mechanism for automatic self-regulation of which we know is that of the competition of very large numbers of producers; that is to say, the sort of business structure which the nineteenth-century business man and economist assumed (and still assume) to exist. The alternative is to accept American business as it now is and to attempt to design a set of mechanisms which will do some of the work of the automatically self-regulating features which have been lost,—or which never existed.

It is useless to disguise the fact that either course of action is likely to be enormously difficult; and it is idle to attempt to say which, could it be carried out with the utmost intelligence and thoroughness, would lead to the more fruitful economic order. We do not know. But of the two possible approaches some modification of the present order of things is likely to prove more practical than the institution of a model radically different from the present structure.

We have already seen that the sort of competition which is automatic and self-regulating is an exceedingly special form of competition indeed. To institute this form of competition we should have to face the question of breaking up industrial units to an extent hitherto imagined by few. Our task would not be one of finding monopolies and dissolving them, nor would we be much concerned with combinations, gentlemen's agreements and price leadership. But it would be necessary to search out any scale of production which gave evidence of present or potential power to the individual producer to exercise jurisdiction over his prices. To remove this power in our important industries the individual units would have to be made small indeed. In less important industries,—where there is now 'large scale' production, also,—the individual units would be minute. Whether they could make efficient use of modern methods of production may be seriously doubted.

Half-way measures in efforts to restore self-regulative competition will not suffice; an incomplete jurisdiction of producers over prices, we have seen, may lead to consequences as unsatisfactory as more complete controls.[1] It is difficult to see how one could lessen the degree of jurisdiction one now finds in the women's garments trades, the needle trades, and the laundry trade. And it is precisely here at present that the necessity for setting prices without the power to make price control effective is at least partly responsible for price wars, low wages and cut-throat competition. Surely there is nothing that can be done to sub-divide the units further in such industries, and nothing that could be accomplished were they subdivided. At the other extreme there are industries where it is hopeless to expect that self-regulative competition can be made effective. This is already recognized in the case of railroads and communications, light and power utilities and milk distribution. It is not so generally recognized, but is, nevertheless, true of such industries as shipbuilding, locomotive construction, and others. It is fantastic to suppose that we would ever take actual steps to reduce to anywhere near 'atomistic' proportions the unit scale of operations in the manufacture of automobiles or farm implements, or steel; unit costs would certainly go to impossible levels. We have seen, also, that

1. See pp. 36-43.

there are lines of activity, notably retailing and the distributive trades generally, where mere numbers of operations give no assurance of optimum output at low cost,—in fact, numbers are more likely to mean diluted business and inefficient operation.

The most dubious aspect of an effort to restore regulative competition is that it seeks to 'restore' something which has never existed in most modern industry. When most human activity was devoted to the production of food and to the handicraft manufacture of clothing, a degree of regulative competition among many small producing units somewhat similar to modern staple agriculture may have existed, although even then it was limited by the royal monopolies in raw materials and the regulations of the guilds. But, as the standard of living has become higher and more varied in content, production of food and clothing has become less important relative to the production of all goods. Farm production, and some of the subsequent manufacture of food and clothing, still show characteristics of self-regulating competition. But of the wide variety of other industries which produce for modern needs many were cast from their beginning in a different mold, and in many of the remainder the competition of large numbers disappeared before the industry grew out of the stage of experimental adolescence.[1] To attempt to re-institute regulative competition would be to impose upon much of American industry a wholly new and untried form

1. For example, the automobile industry had many times the present number of individual manufacturers in the pre-war years, but nowhere near enough for *regulative* competition.

of organization. To achieve self-regulative competition American industry would have to undergo major surgery.

If we do not or cannot return to the regulation of 'atomistic' competition, how are we to re-design and supplement the organization of modern industry to provide that degree of regulation which is so obviously essential? How, in other words, is it to be made to operate more nearly at capacity or optimum output with less unemployment, with freedom from price warfare at the expense of employee groups and, most important of all, with a lessened susceptibility to booms and depressions? Further, what changes are to be made in the corporation, the unit in modern industrial organization, so that a management which responds to the individual profit motive will, by so doing, contribute to the welfare of the community?

We would not expect to find any one formula for achieving these objectives; in any case we have not sought for one. The attack we propose is a frankly piecemeal affair which works upon not one but several fronts. We do not pretend that our suggestions on each of the several fronts are the best possible, or that in total they would eliminate all the weaknesses in our present industrial organization. We shall be content if they do two things,—if they demonstrate that practical steps can be taken, and point the way to further progress.

CHAPTER VIII
Industrial Publicity

THE first proposal which is directly or indirectly related to others made below is that secrecy be swept from the widest possible area of American business. Specifically, it is proposed that gradually, but as rapidly as practicable, production, sales, prices, earnings, assets and liabilities, intercorporate stockholdings, employment, wages and hours, regularly be reported. We suggest special machinery for the reporting and release of this information.

Strictly speaking there is no such thing as private business; nothing upon which the welfare and happiness of 130,000,000 people depends can possibly be a private affair. But we do not base our suggestion for publicity on an abstract conception of this sort,—rather we base it on the practical view that sound national progress and sound business growth alike are made on the basis of knowledge and not on guesswork. No business man worthy of the name is without up-to-the-minute information concerning his sales, costs, earnings, and cash position. His decisions, large and small, are made on the basis of such information. Yet at the same time we expect our legislators,—national and state,—to make complex and difficult decisions on economic matters with but the sketchiest of information. At any given time we do not know at what level the national plant is producing and to get at the past record of physical volume of production we must depend on piecemeal estimates. Until recently we had no knowledge of the national income, i.e., the earnings of the national plant, and there is a goodly range of possible error in present national income estimates. Our data on employment and payrolls are far from satisfactory. We pass tax legislation using broad estimates about the taxable base. We legislate for the unemployed without knowing the extent and character of the unemployment, our guesses as to numbers of unemployed sometimes differ by millions. Yet even when banks are not closed or half the population in economic straits, there *must* be economic legislation,—or dictation. The requirements of existing economic legislation demand that we put an end to our wasteful and unbusinesslike lack of information on the nation's business. The changes,—'backward' and 'forward,'—which are sure to be made in the future double this demand. In the battle for economic progress we need better information to hold the present trenches, or even to retire in fair order. We cannot content ourselves with complaints of the mediocrity of our legislation when we supply our government with such a meagre basis for its decisions.

The case for industrial publicity can be won, we believe, solely on the ground that it is essential for improved economic legislation and improved administration of present laws. The case does not rest there, however. There are other advantages to be cited.

Labor stands to gain from increased publicity on wage and working conditions. So long as the worker is ignorant of the alternative opportunities in other places of employment, he has little or no mobility. He cannot leave his job to investigate wages and hours elsewhere. Hear-say and rumor are not safe substitutes for straight-forward information. In good times, anyhow, full information would make possible a degree of discrimination by the worker against the sub-standard employer; it is such discrimination which is implicitly relied upon by the theory underlying self-regulative competition but which never has been exercised and never could be without sufficient and authentic information. If it is argued that the individual worker would not use such data it is still reasonable to reply that the trade unions would. And publicity for the sub-standard employer would be a healthy thing in itself.

The business man himself has a plea to make for better business information. One rarely needs to look far from his own door for some plant or enterprise that is a monument to an error in business judgment. Plants are erected to stand idle because business men and investors are not aware that competitors are expanding, also; or they are not aware that the industry itself is declining or that its center of gravity is shifting to other areas. Labor and capital are devoted to the multiplication of retailing establishments when returns do not justify the existing investment in the industry. Full information in these instances would be a warning sign to both outsiders and insiders. Similarly, although the case is a less obvious one, it is probable that investors and business men occasionally forego favorable returns and consumers pay relatively high prices because the possibilities for profitable competition in a given line are not generally known. In any event better information would lead to a distribution of new investment more in line with the needs of society.

Finally, we would confidently expect an improvement in business management with full information. Waste could be prevented and much misdirected energy saved if business managers could guide their policies with their eyes mostly open instead of mostly shut. Not only would the present generation of managers be helped, but any reduction in the proportion of guesswork to reason in management problems would provide more accurate standards for appraising managers and management, and might be expected to bring into the field a larger number of able men.

By those who hanker to 'restore' the automatic competitive system pictured by classical economics and used in arguing a defense for non-interference, a suggestion for complete publicity must be welcomed. For that is precisely what classical economists assumed to exist.[1] Those who wish to start with things as they are and believe some regulation inevitable, but who want the least which will serve its essential purposes, must agree that the more publicity we can have the less regulation we shall have to have. For

1. Thus the most prominent English economist in the classical tradition in the present century has concluded that 'There is clearly room for improvement in the matter of business publicity, and, if such improvement were made, ignorance would be lessened, equality in the values of marginal net products promoted, and the size of the national dividend thereby increased.' A.C.Pigou, *Economics of Welfare*, 3d Edition, 1929.

publicity means that the community has an opportunity to judge things for itself by standards of the communal good. Hence, publicity itself becomes a good regulator.

We realize that the suggestions we are making for industrial publicity will take many years to get in full working order. A variety of practical considerations will indicate what sorts of information should be made public first and which later on. Ultimately we would like to see the following sorts of information available, and would hope to see common sense guide the selection of what should be undertaken as first steps and how steady, even, if slow, progress can best be maintained.

(1) *Production, Inventories, and Sales.* Reports on production, sales, unfilled orders, and inventories of finished goods are a first essential in the program for industrial publicity. These reports must be steadily extended over the widest possible range of industry, beginning with the most important materials not now recorded, and should be freely available to all.

Information on inventories and dealers' stocks is of particular importance throughout the distributive trades. Practical considerations, no doubt, set limits to the number or completeness of the reports on sales and inventories which could be required from small retail enterprises. The same is true of production and sales reports from very small manufacturers and from agriculture. We feel, however, that such considerations should be the only ones limiting the scope of this phase of the industrial publicity program.

From all firms and all industries the reports should be as frequent as may be practical from the point of view of the administering body and the reporting firms. For some industries (electric power production, carloadings, and steel orders and production) weekly reports are entirely possible. For the great bulk of industry, monthly or quarterly reports would have to serve. In certain cases (e.g., small retailing) reports could not be more frequent than once or twice a year. Here, as elsewhere, the program would have to be carefully adjusted to the circumstances of the industry.[1]

Save, perhaps, for data on employment, wages and hours, no information is so necessary for a month to month check on the functioning of the economic machinery as that which covers production and inven-

1. Total inventories in the United States at any given time are estimated by the National Bureau of Economic Research to vary from 60% to 75% of the annual flow of goods to consumers. By drawing upon inventory, then, we could stop the wheels of industry practically dead for a month or two; by replenishing we could drive them overtime. Clearly it is of the utmost importance for business men and everyone else to know whether and to what extent an increase in orders is filling an inventory or a consumer demand. (From an unpublished manuscript by Simon Kuznets.) (See Table)

Average Inventory as a percentage of the annual flow of goods to consumer

	Current Price	'29 Prices		Current Price	'29 Prices
1919	71%	63	1927	62%	60
1920	68	71.5	1928	60	60
1921	75.5	77	1929	58	59
1922	68.5	70	1930	62	66
1923	65	66.5	1931	65	73
1924	68	66	1932	67	76
1925	65	63	1933	63.5	70
1926	61	62			

tories. It would give us timely and reasonably accurate data on our national income and simplify greatly the problems of short run business forecasting. It is a serious reflection on our national business acumen that we have continued so long with isolated bits or inadequate substitutes for the information here recommended.

(2) *Prices.* We recommend full price publicity for all industries where the number of products or sellers of lines make it feasible. By full publicity we mean publicity of lists, quantity discounts, quality differentials, rebates and other modifications of list prices. The reporting of prices should follow closely on any price change and the reported prices should be available (as all other information) to competitors, buyers, and the public. There should be no attempt to disguise the identity of the firm which quotes any particular price.

It is frankly recognized that this recommendation strikes upon a much debated question of modern industrial policy—the question of open price reporting. A surprising amount of confused thinking and misinformation has been contributed both to the support of and the attack on open pricing.[1] To suppose, as some have

1. It is a question, also, which has been the subject for lengthy although somewhat inconclusive investigation. Cf. *Open Price Trade Associations.* Report of the Federal Trade Commission, 70th Congress, 2d Session 1929.

The studies of the price-effects of various kinds of codes are mostly inconclusive. The fever of high expectation of the spring of 1933 and the consequent sub-normal fall caused a changing market which made it hard to say what effects were of codes and what of markets. The comparisons with pre-code days were mostly invalidated by ignorance of the actual extent and methods which had characterized specific pre-code cases of price-reporting, and often of whether such reporting

done, that open price agreements lead to the same technical market perfection as may be found in the wheat market is plainly foolish. The two forms of competition cannot be compared, for in the wheat market there is no producer jurisdiction over prices and with or without open price associations, in modern industry there will still be a large degree of such jurisdiction. At the other extreme, it is equally foolish to suppose that prices open to all sellers and all buyers will immediately rise and thereafter be either rigid or rising.

The controversy over open pricing reached a high temperature when N.R.A. codes were being set up, and it involved thousands of men who had never had occasion to think of the problem before. The hottest fight was around the question of requiring advances of prices to be reported some days or weeks before they were to take effect. Most of the fighters assumed that prices would be open to sellers only, as in some of the 'open-price associations' of pre-N.R.A. times. Generally, as always in so sudden a controversy, the evil and good were announced as ruin and salvation, it was 'whole hog or none,' and all businesses alike.

Fortunately for present purposes much of the controversy over open pricing is irrelevant. In the first place we are not proposing advance reporting of prices either with or without a waiting period. In the second place it is our hypothesis that the number of producers and the

existed or not. The studies would in any case not invalidate our hypothesis that the principal conditioning factor of specific price behavior is the sort of goods you are dealing with. If they make certain uniformities and stabilities easy, an association may develop and hold together. If not, it probably won't.

market character of goods are the primary determinants of price behavior. Hence, open prices will have their principal effect in producing price uniformity, i.e., in reducing secret discriminations. In the third place we are not proposing prices that are open to sellers alone, but prices that are open to buyers and the public. Finally, we are not proposing price reporting as an isolated measure. It is an important part of what we believe to be a fairly comprehensive program of business publicity. To proceed with other types of publicity and to suppress price information would be incongruous.

There are industries where any sort of price reporting is probably impractical or not worth the effort involved. Such is the case where there are a large number of scattered units as in small service industries and in some lines of retailing. With this proposal, as with the others, the whole program could not be put into effect at once. It is good sense to start with the most feasible and more important matters and move steadily onward until practical considerations of a genuine nature intervene.

(3) *Financial Statements and Statements of Earnings.* Publicity on assets and liabilities and on earnings and losses should be complete. Not only can any business be managed more wisely and sanely, with eyes open to the condition of customers and competitors, but the useful investment of capital in new enterprises practically demands such knowledge. Eventually statements should be filed quarterly for all corporations in all industries, and for all private concerns and partnerships of significant size. Earnings reports should show earnings (or deficit) for the previous quarters and previous year with com-

parisons. In the case of integrated corporations the financial statement and the record of earnings should be rendered both for the individual concerns and as a consolidated statement.

More progress has been made in getting full publicity on assets and liabilities and on earnings than on any other factors in modern business. Even here, however, we have scarcely begun. Just enough has been done to indicate the wisdom and desirability of completing the job.

(4) *Inter-Corporate Stock Ownership and Director and Management Ownership.* The cross currents of ownership and control in the modern corporate structure, as we have seen, have come to have important effects upon the way the economic system functions. They are effects which are important to the welfare of the community at large. For this reason we suggest quarterly reports by all corporations on their holdings in other corporations. Of equal importance, as part of the same report, a statement should be made of the holdings of corporation officers and directors in other enterprises where these holdings are of significant amount.

(5) *Wages and Hours and Employment.* Quarterly reports on wages, wage rates and hours for various classes of employees, and the average number employed in each class during each quarter should be developed. Under the heading of employees there should be included the salaried officers and executives. We propose that this information be made public for individual concerns, though some exceptions would be necessary to reduce administrative and statistical work. Concerns

with less than three to five employees would probably
have to be omitted or reported only in census years; if
this exception was not made the cost of administering
the publicity provision for a host of small proprietary
and agricultural enterprises would be burdensome. We
believe it is essential, however, that this information,
like the foregoing, be regularly available over the largest
practicable section of industry.

The Machinery for Industrial Publicity

Careful attention must be given the machinery for administering a program of industrial publicity and every
effort should be made to consolidate and systematize
the reports required. It is useless to suppose that it could
be so arranged that there will be no additional burden on
the individual firm, although it is to be noted that our
emphasis is largely on information which is now a matter of record within the concerns. There should certainly be some reasonable tolerance of variations in the
manner of presenting information as between individual
firms and particularly as between industries. Further-
more, an effort should be made to have the comprehensive publicity program as here proposed replace the
piecemeal or isolated reports now required or requested
by the government.

In administering a program for industrial publicity
considerable use can and should be made of trade
association machinery now organized in part for a
similar purpose. We suggest that in legislating for the
broad outlines of a program for industrial publicity,
Congress designate the government department and

bureau to direct the work and give formal recognition to the trade association as a co-operating agency. When an industry through its trade association meets standards of accuracy, completeness and promptness specified by Congress and the executive bureau in charge, firms would file the required information in duplicate with the trade association and one copy would be filed by the association with the government. Both the material at the trade association headquarters and in Washington would be open to public inspection. The trade association and the government would decide which information called for by the law should be published within the associations or more widely. Recalcitrant firms within an industry, and industries without an effective trade association would be subject to the direct jurisdiction of the government. No enforcement powers need be delegated to the trade association.

INDUSTRIAL PUBLICITY AND COMPETITION

Under the proposal which we are making more of any one business man's affairs will be revealed to his competitors than is revealed at present, and the business man will know an equivalent amount more about the affairs of his competitors. The competitive position of the various members of the industry would theoretically remain unchanged. As a matter of fact there would be some changes, certain of them of a wholly desirable sort. At the present time some concerns, most commonly the larger ones in an industry, have means for finding out what they wish to know about a competitor particularly if it is a smaller firm. Such advantages, gained by methods which involve questionable standards of ethics, would be removed. But we see no reason for protecting gains based on use of spies and stool pigeons in competitors' plants. Likewise, we do not seek to protect those who engage in secret labor or price practices which they would not follow in public.

But if publicity is not to alter relative competitive positions unfairly, it must be general. In all industries where it is applied it must sooner or later cover all members of the industry. One competitor must not be required to make his production public while another keeps his secret. It is for this reason among others, of course, that industrial publicity must be compulsory.

So far as we are aware the case for business secrecy rests on two grounds. The first of these is that the firm will be more assiduous in its search for new methods and processes if it is to enjoy exclusive return from these for a period. It is apparent that nothing in our recommendations bears upon this argument. The patent protection of the private firm remains undisturbed and it is under no compulsion to make public secret methods or processes. The second argument for business secrecy is that competitors receive an unfair advantage if one's business information is made freely available to them. We have just stated our belief that this argument does not apply when business publicity is general.

It is not likely that business as a whole has selfish reasons for wishing to conceal the sort of information we have just outlined, provided furnishing such information is made general. Where there are such reasons, we have no alternative but to conclude that these very reasons are the strongest possible argument for publicity.

Consumers Goods Publicity

There is one final field for publicity which is set apart somewhat from the rest and where we believe it will be necessary for the government to take the lead in making the information available to a greater extent than in the types of industrial information we have just mentioned. We refer to publicity on grades, qualities and standards of consumer goods. It is ignorance in this field which gives countenance to a part of the wasteful sales competition, large-scale advertising expenditure, and extravagant claims and counter-claims which go to make up the costly structure of modern selling. For if the consumer is unaware of the true qualities of the goods he is buying, then he is fair game for all who have a chance of taking advantage of him. The purveyor of bad goods, if the consumer is ignorant, has as good an opportunity as the seller of better quality merchandise. The seller of honest goods must spend money and effort in self defense. If, as more frequently happens, qualities are the same, each seller must spend to hold his position against the others.

The escape from this wasteful circle is to give the consumer the facts; when two brands of gasoline are the same, the consumer should be told so. If this were done there might well follow a marked decline in the claims and counter claims for rival products; for firms only spend money convincing people who are capable of being convinced.

The machinery for consumer publicity could start naturally with an extension of present government work on grades and standards. Progress has already been made in the Bureau of Standards and in the Department of Agriculture, but enlargement of these services would be highly desirable.

T. W. Schults

CHAPTER IX
Regulation

THE crux of the subject of public regulation of business
has never been whether or not there should be regulation. It has always been a question of the kind of regulation there should be and of its objectives. The business
man who pleads for freedom from government regulation does not desire the repeal of all public supervision
and control of economic life. Patent laws, laws of con-
tract and their enforcement, and tariffs are government
controls which business men would not care to abolish.

We have been speaking much in the preceding pages
of regulative competition. The term suggests that the
form of regulation which accompanies such competition
is of a special sort, and this is indeed the case. Where
regulative or 'pure' competition obtains and industry is
so organized (or is presumed to be so organized) that it
tends toward a moving equilibrium of optimum or high
efficiency output, full employment, and constant search
for greater efficiency and technological improvement,
then any regulation by the state must follow a special
design. Broadly it must be the kind of regulation and
only the kind that promotes the condition of equilibrium
or balance. Or, to change the metaphor, it must be the
sort of regulation which oils the machinery, meshes un-
meshed gears, and which, perhaps, reinforces certain

structurally weak parts. The regulation must not, however, alter the machine itself, attempt to change its speed, or interfere with new departures in design.

In nineteenth century England and late nineteenth and early twentieth century America, the theory, if not the fact, of self-regulative competition held general sway. In England and America there was a fairly consistent adherence to the kind of public regulation appropriate to this competition. The state oiled the machinery in various ways. It protected property, enforced contracts, adjusted disputes between employers, and insisted on minimum standards of business honesty. These functions were regarded by many as the greatest permissible range of public activity. Competition was assumed to do the remainder of the regulating.

The state, however, was gradually forced to accept a larger measure of responsibility. Yielding to the view that the private individual is structurally weak as the unit for doing business, it fostered and protected the joint stock company or corporation. Certain labor groups (notably women and children), seemed likely to be squeezed or mangled by the machine. The state came to their aid. In America the design of the machine was altered to a considerable extent by tariff protection. In both England and America there came gradually to be marked out an area where self-regulating, self-adjusting competition could not work or could not be trusted. Into this breach, likewise, the state stepped. Railroads and light and water utilities were either necessarily monopolies, or else competition, if it did exist, took on a peculiarly violent and uncertain form. The state found it necessary in the interest of the railroads and utilities, and the users of their services, to set and enforce prices. In the case of banks, fiduciaries and the professions, the occasional debauches which characterized all self-regulative competition were so dangerous to the community that some regulation there was necessary.

In America there was a Frankenstein complex, also, which gave rise to another and quite distinct form of regulation. It was feared that some part of the machine would one day get out of control and presently rise up and devour the rest of it. Drive shafts, pistons, bolts, nuts, and buzz saws and even consumers would all go down the hungry maw of this monster. The monster, of course, was monopoly—monopoly in the absolute sense—and once out of hand it was feared that monopoly would be more likely to control the country than be controlled by it. Since the very existence of a self-regulating machine depended on keeping monopoly under control, it was safe to do some redesigning of parts to keep it down. The Sherman Act in the eighties, followed by the Federal Trade Commission Act, the Clayton Act, and last of all the Robinson-Patman Act, were all aimed in varying degree at monopoly. But we have seen that it is not '100% monopolies,' or even firms controlling 51% of the industry, but a growth of single producers to sizes large enough (perhaps 5%) to affect price appreciably which is the basic factor in eliminating the self-regulating character of industry. This misdirection of legislative emphasis is understandable, however, because attention was inevitably centered on the well-known power of the monopoly to engage in exploitative price practices.

It is plain that even when self-regulative competition was assumed to exist, a considerable amount of regulation was necessary, including regulation that sought to maintain competition. Naturally, however, the disappearance from modern industry of so much self-regulative competition has made this type of regulation inadequate. The present task, therefore, is not to improve the machinery for doing an old and familiar job. It is to invent new machinery for a new job.

We can conveniently break our suggestions on public regulation into two parts. First we consider the problem of regulation where competition has been and is by some still assumed to be the regulative force, but where in fact the characteristics of competition which might make it self-regulative are gone forever. Next we survey in a brief and general way the regulation which has long been applied to railroads, utilities, and like industries where it was early recognized that competition was not a satisfactory regulator in itself.

GENERAL INDUSTRIAL REGULATION

In suggesting a program for industrial regulation we are faced at the outset with the fact that we do not yet know with any degree of precision the form which that regulation should take or the techniques it should employ. There has been no lack of discussion of regulation; perhaps one difficulty is that there has been so much discussion which lacked a careful definition of terms and a rigorous scrutiny of the issues of principle and practice which regulation involves. In addition, we had for two years in the N.R.A. the beginnings of a large scale experiment in at least one phase of industrial regulation. But none of this is enough as yet to justify any one attempting to draw a detailed blueprint. For a business structure as varied and complex as that of the United States there can be no simple formula, no easy rule which can be laid down for all. Indeed, in our forty years of floundering anti-trust policy, and in the N.R.A. ineffectiveness and difficulties may be attributed to over-simple formulae and to the effort to apply fixed rules over too wide a variety of industrial conditions.

On the other hand, we are faced with a structure of economy which, if our analysis or our common sense is correct, does not have the power of self-regulation. If industry cannot regulate itself, and if regulation, as we have shown, is necessary in the interest of the community, then the responsibility rests with the state. There is no place else for this responsibility to rest; either the state must make the attempt or we must content ourselves with a policy of drift.

If, therefore, we must regulate and don't yet know how to, we must start as sensibly and safely as possible and learn as we go along. The device we recommend is not regulation *per se*, but exploration of the art or technique of regulation. We must do some rational experimental work in the art of industrial regulation. The first steps might be taken in the case of those industries which have shown in recent years extreme underutilization or extreme fluctuation in use of plant and labor resources; or which have had strikingly high profits combined with unreasonably high or inflexible prices; or which have undergone competitive reduction of labor standards; or which have shown excessively wasteful distributive methods. Exploration in the art of regulation should begin where a lack of regulation at present is producing the most unsatisfactory results.

For practical machinery we suggest that a Commission be empowered by Congress to identify and make the necessary study of industries with a low social performance. On the basis of such study, the Commission would be authorized to invite representatives of the industry to co-operate in formulating a plan for such industrial policies, e.g., such level and such regularity of production and such price and labor policies, as conform to the public interest. If co-operation proves impossible, the Commission should be empowered to prepare such a plan itself.

Upon completion of a plan we think its submission to a technically qualified semi-judicial Board of Review would be desirable. This Board would pass on any disputed points of equity in connection with the plan. When approved by it the Commission would be empowered to put the plan into effect for the industry. Changes in the plan initiated by the Commission and approved by the Board of Review could be made at any time. Changes in or perhaps even discontinuance of the plan could be ordered, also, by the Board of Review at any time.

We do not propose that industry plans be drawn up for all industry within any short space of time. We repeat that this program is an exploration in the art of regulation where regulation appears to be most needed. We do not conceive of the initiative in the adoption of the plan as coming from industry, but rather from the regulating commission. In this sense we look upon the program as a substitute for anti-trust prosecution. Rather than blindly sub-dividing the units in an industry in the faint hope that certain desirable results will come out of the sub-division, we propose that the results be defined and a program be laid out directly to achieve these socially desirable and defined results. It would be hoped that the co-operation of each industry would be obtained in achieving the objectives which the community has the right to expect of it. In the absence of full industry co-operation, however, there would be no choice but to proceed with as much of it as can be gained, or as a last resort without it.

The objectives of the industry plans, like the objectives of regulation itself, are, of course, enlarged and regularized output and the maintenance of such price policies, labor standards, and earnings as would place the industry in the best relation to the welfare of the community. But even these are not matters to which we would care to give *a priori* definition. A major task in the development of the art of regulation is the appraisal of specific industrial policies in their relation to the general welfare.

For effecting its objectives it is important that the Commission be provided with the widest practical variety of tools. It should not be bound by any narrow concept of order-giving in the regulation which it undertakes. In certain instances tariff adjustment might well be an appropriate and effective means to the desired ends; in certain cases yardstick competition would be a desirable tool; subsidy as a means of directing economic resources should certainly be one of the tools of the Commission. It is possible that with Congressional consent taxation might be used. That it have such a variety of measures at hand is essential; for, always granting the need of proper safeguards, it would be through working with a goodly assortment of tools that the Commission would develop its techniques of regulation.

Certain interpretations of the constitution doubtless stand in the way of this program although we do not pretend to say whether or not these interpretations are likely to be the ruling ones. But since the only function of the law is to serve man we do not believe in being stopped by objections of a purely legal sort—at least so long as we have means for revising laws to meet the ends we seek.

While a Commission is studying the industries which society most needs to have regulated and is making its first experiments, there should be thrown open to the rest of the business world the chance to develop the technique of self-regulation under government supervision. This could take several of the forms which in recent years have been discussed as fair-trade practice agreements. They make legal such agreements as a significant majority—say two-thirds or three-fourths—of a trade or industry may work out and such as may be approved by a department of the government as of net value to the country as a whole.

These self-regulatory experiments could not be ex-

pected to go very far,—certainly not at first. For without
any plan to coerce the ten per cent or more who would
surely stay out no tackling of the more important wasteful abuses in present trade practices would be possible.
But much underbrush might be cleared away; and in
any case work under such agreements would be an education in the realities of business.

UTILITY REGULATION

We come now to that important area of industry where
public regulation has been taken for granted, but where
past regulation has been guided not by the objectives
which we hold up for a well-ordered industrial community but rather by the special or exceptional role
which these industries were assumed to play in a society
which was left more largely to itself.

The unworkmanlike character of our regulation of
light, power, communication and transportation in the
past is pretty well known. Rate bases have been com-
pounded out of such confused concepts as original investment, cost of reproduction and use value together
with a generous admixture of guesswork and horse-
trading. The return on the valuation so established has
been governed partly by considerations of 'fair return'
and the 'going rate,' partly by the level of past or customary earnings, and sometimes by political pressure,
intimidation, and propaganda. When once established,
increases in rate schedules have been fought by users or
consumers and decreases have been fought by the companies. Strength and strategy in battle have often
counted for more than economic criteria in settling the

level of rates. During the 1920's, a band of holding company adventurers spun the power companies into a series of vast corporate cobwebs, and 1930's efforts to untangle these cobwebs were put down as attacks on liberty. We have come to think of our efforts to regulate, at least in certain of those fields where it has been necessary, as a rather messy piece of work.

But, this regulation has on the whole been consistent with our current ideas of the exceptional nature of regulation. Property rights in the regulated industries were assiduously protected and the level of earnings was the thing around which the regulation turned. So long as regulation permitted favorable earnings, the utilities were assured of their share of investment funds for growth and expansion. Nothing else was thought to be as important as this; and in a pioneering, growing country the thought was often right on balance. Any regulation of public service companies would be certain to take this special form if it was considered to apply only to the exceptions in an economy which, by a system of checks and balances, kept itself in a well-regulated path of moderation and progress.

The old objectives of curbing or moderating exploitation of the public and providing for some rate of expansion must give way to an entirely new concept of rail, utility, and similar regulation. We must aim fairly and squarely at the objective of so regulating 'utilities' that they make their maximum contribution to community welfare in the broadest sense of the term.

We do not attempt to draw up a bill of particulars on public utility regulation for we are not competent to do

so and our concern is first of all with a changed attitude.
We would like to see enlarged Federal control particularly of interstate concerns. We also believe that a slowly increased public ownership will prove to be desirable.
Needless to say we endorse efforts to work out something in the way of a comprehensive plan of development in the power field. What we would most like to
see is an approach to the whole problem of the regulated
industries which is based on the view that this is one
part of a larger job and which has as its goals the full
functioning of the economic system for the public
welfare.

Our idea of utility regulation covers, of course, increased service, wider utilization of services and the
lowest cost consistent with the provision of that amount
of utility services, in comparison with the amount of
other useful things, that people want. Present regulation
with its emphasis on earnings rather than on output, does
not achieve these ends. But this part of the task is not
difficult, at least in principle. A strong regulating commission, particularly if it had such devices as subsidy,
yardstick competition and the like at its command,
would have a fairly well-marked path to follow. Modern utility regulation, however, must do something
more. It must see that railroad rates, and power rates, 'fit
in' or mesh with the working of the rest of the economic system. An example will illustrate the point. During the past depression railroad freight rates conformed
not at all to the general downward movement in prices
from 1929 on, in fact there was an increase in rates in
1931. Obviously, very little attention was given by the

regulating bodies to the question whether rigid or increased freight rates made worse or better the health of a very sick economic system. Modern utility regulation and likewise modern industrial regulation must take account of such matters for they are of major importance. Perhaps we shall find it wise in future depressions to slash rail rates deeply and make it up to the roads by subsidy. With the wider concept of regulation we are suggesting here, the determination of such a reduction of rates would take into account its effect upon easing a depression, just as an increase of rates would be considered as one means of checking a boom. But so long as regulation looks largely at the effect on utility earnings as at present such useful possibilities will never be considered.

WAGES AND HOURS REGULATION

We have drawn attention to the tendency of much modern competition to degenerate into competitive decreases of wages and increases of hours.[1] While it is perfectly true that the result of this process may sometimes be the production of goods at low cost, we have no hesitation in concluding that such an accounting is inadequate. The magnitude of the suffering which is

---

1. The technically trained reader will observe that we have not raised the larger question of the remuneration of the worker under conditions of other than self-regulative competition. The omission may appear particularly striking in view of the theoretically well-established argument that under such conditions he receives less than the value of his marginal product. But in defining the scope of the problem at hand we have (perhaps arbitrarily) eliminated questions concerning the distribution of incomes from our analysis and the larger questions of wage and trade union policy from our suggestions.

caused by competitive wage reduction and stretching out of hours of work is imponderable, but no one can doubt that it is great. In many cases it is necessary for the community to enter upon a bare-faced direct relief subsidy to supplement the wages of an industry which have become inadequate for family support. From a purely mathematical point of view the burden which low wages puts upon the communities in which low wage industries are to be found is as truly a part of cost of manufacture as if the employer carried it. In the same category is the subsequent cost of caring for a population whose health or morale has been wrecked by competitively reduced wage standards.

We do not wish to imply that low wages are always forced by the modern conditions of competition in industry. In many cases labor is able to protect itself and there are employers who resist the pressure to reduce wages. But since industry is so organized that most concerns must follow where only a small minority of wage-cutters lead, the situation to which we are calling attention is sufficiently important to warrant general action.

There is nothing novel about the proposal we make,— It is for carefully worked out minimum wage legislation and hours regulation by the Federal Government, these to be applicable to the widest practicable area of American industry. We are by no means unaware of the objections, legal and economic, which are commonly raised to wages and hours legislation. To the legal difficulties in the way there is but one answer,—one which we have already given. The law must serve the achievement of human ends, not obstruct the process. The economic objections mostly hinge on the introduction of a new rigidity into our economic system. We grant, of course, that a new rigidity will be introduced, but we do not grant the importance of this innovation. To begin with the proposal is only that there be a floor to wage reductions; it is not proposed to fix all wages. In the second place, we do not propose that these standards be sweeping or arbitrary. We assume that they are to be worked out for individual industries, with, no doubt, some regional differentials within industries. This means that no industry will be confronted with the problem of meeting a suddenly increased and inexorably fixed wages bill. In the case of industries which have distressingly low wage standards at the time that the legislation is passed we would favor provision for a period of gradual readjustment.

Finally, we now have much rigidity and it is deeply seated in our system. We see no possible hope of eliminating it and reinstating a self-regulative mechanism. Hence new influences which may increase rigidity must be examined as to their chances of net good but cannot be rejected without hearing. We believe that most people who argue against minimum wage and hour legislation because of their possible effects in stiffening prices would be slow to recommend the lines of action necessary to make prices in the steel industry, or the aluminum industry, purely and truly flexible. Under such circumstances we do not feel that on technical grounds labor can be denied the protection of hours and wages legislation.

CHAPTER X
Corporation Policy

WE are of the opinion that any program designed to place modern industry on a more workable and fruitful basis must extend to the structure of the corporation. We recognize, of course, the advantages of the corporate form of business organization under our system and its contribution to the general material welfare. At the same time, we know that the modern corporation has developed certain features which hamper orderly industrial progress,—features which circumscribe and even misdirect the profit motive. Fortunately, there are some remedies which are worth trying—remedies which can be applied and yet leave unaltered the essential outlines of modern corporate organization. There are many who assert that the modern corporation is in need of major surgery; and it is possible that they are right; but it is also possible that a number of lesser operations will restore it to a condition of comparatively good health as measured by social standards.

The maze of conflicting and (still worse) competing state corporation statutes is the first matter for attention. For this there is a simple and fairly obvious remedy— Federal incorporation,—at least for corporations above a certain size, or which have some pre-determined degree of interstate ownership or commerce. Stockholders, and other security holders, legitimate corporate business itself, and the public, all have much to gain from placing corporate enterprise under a single, comprehensive, strict, and at the same time fair and equitable corporation statute. The present situation, where no single state can seek to improve its corporation laws without risking a migration of its corporations and the attendant revenue to some other state, is untenable.

While Federal incorporation could facilitate most of the steps listed below, some of them are independent of it.

1. There should be a fairly drastic simplification of corporation structure. The only criterion by which complex holding company arrangements, deviously interrelated subsidiaries and the like can be justified is that of service to the public. The complexity of many of our present corporate enterprises cannot be so justified.

2. The present degree of separation of the stockholder ownership from the control of the modern large corporation is an accomplished fact and it seems highly impractical to seek to overcome it. But if we grant this to be the case we must recognize that the directorate of our larger corporate enterprises is actually in a fiduciary capacity for security holders. We believe that the law should recognize them as trustees and accord them the measure of supervision accorded generally to those who act as fiduciaries. If the security holder (and the public) must accept the officers of a corporation 'on trust,' there should be proper machinery for making certain

that such trust is honorably discharged. It is to the interest of those corporation officers who now hold to high standards of corporate practice that their standards be made universal.

3. The scarcity of managerial talent in the United States is not so great that any single individual should need to serve on from a half dozen to a score or more of boards of directors. Subject to carefully drawn exceptions, therefore, every board member should be required to devote his attention exclusively to one or at most a very limited number of concerns. We regard this measure as a method of focussing managerial and directorial talent more sharply on the affairs of a particular corporation; as a means of increasing the range of opportunity in corporation control; and, most important, as an eventual curb on the sort of intercorporate dealing which is to the advantage of directors mutual to two corporations, but is at the expense of the stockholders and general public.

4. As a further curb on intercorporate dealing the law should prohibit officers or directors of any concern from holding more than a defined amount of stock in another concern where business between the two concerns exceeds a carefully defined limit.

5. The purchase and sale by officers and directors of a corporation of securities of their own concern should be made a matter of record and restricted by law with a view to prohibiting speculative dealing by the individuals in control.

6. Finally, we endorse the developments of recent years

in providing better supervision over security issues. There should be constant improvement along these lines to the point where the public has every assurance of the good faith and honesty of promotors of corporate enterprise.

We dissent from efforts to meet the problems of the modern corporation by reducing its size. Arbitrary measures to prevent bigness *per se* we regard not so much harmful as merely lacking a reasoned and defined objective. No one, we believe, has any clear idea of what discriminatory taxation of the large unit, limitations on the maximum size of corporations, or dissolution of large units would actually accomplish. To make a clear case that it would result in net good would be difficult indeed. One exception is the case of the holding company—investment trust structure. Where adventurers in corporate finance have, with comparatively small or negligible investment of their own, brought a large domain of railroads, utilities, or like properties under their control, a halt should be called. Limitations on the Insul-Van Sweringen species of corporate growth would appear to be entirely in order. Much of this sort of growth would be prevented by a thoroughgoing simplification of corporation structure as suggested above.

CHAPTER XI
A Concluding Note

WE conclude with a brief summary of our central thesis. In the earlier chapters we have attempted to show how far our present economic system has departed from the simple model which was supposed to be a self-regulating mechanism. We have outlined the shortcomings, wastes and strains of a system which operates without these self-regulating features, and for which self-regulation no adequate substitute has been designed.

The substitution of the type of industrial organization which would allow self-regulation we consider costly and impractical and a more drastic step than most people would be willing to stomach. The alternative is to attempt effective modification of the existing organization of industry.

We believe that as a first step business operations should be brought into the broad daylight and we look upon this, of itself, as a wholesome influence in encouraging what is good and discouraging what is unwholesome in the business world, and thus as reducing the extent to which regulation need go.

But there is much to be done in developing fundamentally necessary regulating devices and techniques. Hence, we suggest means for an experimental, but fairly rapid development of techniques of regulation. This should be individually adjusted to different industries and should be aimed specifically at attaining and maintaining the optimum in output and in regularity of output. We believe we shall never learn how to regulate well except by doing it.

We suggest the setting and enforcing of minimum standards of wages and hours. Finally, we offer some amendments to corporation structure to check or remove present tendencies of a harmful or unsocial sort.

Naturally, we do not feel that these measures, however carefully they may be legislated and administered, will 'solve' the problem of instability and below par performance in the economic system. Monetary and banking policies, taxation, direct provision for unemployment and the provision for social security all rank in importance with the measures we are suggesting. There are perhaps some contradictions in our present system which will not yield to any attack consistent with the maintenance of the structure itself. But the battle to preserve democratic institutions against the forces turned loose by the closing of frontiers, by the Great War, and by the forms of modern industrial enterprise may be fairly close. It is plain from our suggestions that we do not belong to the school which cautions democracy to avoid responsibility lest it destroy itself by attempting too much. On the contrary, we are convinced that democracy can best destroy itself by failing to shoulder its responsibilities. We do not believe the democracy can win by remaining forever on the defensive.